STARTING AND RUNNING
A CATERING
BUSINESS

STARTING AND RUNNING
A CATERING BUSINESS

How to start and manage a successful enterprise

CAROL GODSMARK

howtobooks

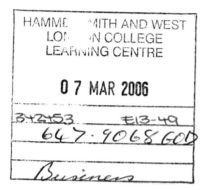
Published by How To Books Ltd
3 Newtec Place, Magdalen Road
Oxford OX4 1RE, United Kingdom.
Tel: (01865) 793806. Fax: (01865) 248780.
info@howtobooks.co.uk
www.howtobooks.co.uk

British Library Cataloguing in Publication Data
A catalogue record for this book is available from the British
Library

Cover design by Baseline Arts Ltd, Oxford
Illustrations by Nicki Averill
Produced for How To Books by Deer Park Productions, Tavistock
Typeset by Pantek Arts Ltd, Maidstone, Kent
Printed and bound by Cromwell Press, Trowbridge, Wiltshire

NOTE: The material contained in this book is set out in good
faith for general guidance and no liability can be accepted for
loss or expense incurred as a result of relying in particular
circumstances on statements made in this book. Laws and
regulations may be complex and liable to change, and readers
should check the current positions with the relevant
authorities before making personal arrangements.

Contents

Acknowledgements

Researching this book has unearthed many enthusiastic, dedicated professional people who have generously contributed their time and expertise and whom I thank most sincerely:

Peter Gladwin, Party Ingredients, London; Ursula Croker, Cook & Buttle, Arundel, West Sussex; Peter Gordon, Providores, London; Jonathan Cooper, Amano Cafe, London; Raymond Blanc and Tracey Clinton, Manoir Aux Quat' Saisons, Oxfordshire; Larry Stone, wine director, Rubicon, San Francisco, California; John Hayler, Planning Department, Chichester District Council, West Sussex; Lawrence Foord and Sarah Parker, Trading Standards, CDC; John White, Environmental Protection, CDC; David Knowles-Ley, Environmental Health, CDC; Julian Mitchell, Christie & Co., London; Brian Duckett and Paul Monaghan, Howath Franchising, London; Lorna and Peter Walters, solicitors, Streathers, London; Simon Henrick, Brake, Tony Lank and Tom Tyrwitt-Drake, The Enterprise Centre, Burgess Hill, West Sussex; Elizabeth Crompton-Batt, Charles Secrett, Mark Haynes and staunch friends and allies Anna Fleming, Chrissie Bates, Jocelyn and Peter Sampson, Caroline Godsmark and others who have shown much patience, goodwill and understanding including Guild of Food Writers co-members.

Many thanks for their wisdom, support and expertise also go to Nikki Read, Giles Lewis, Helen Moreno and Deborah Robinson at How To Books. Melanie Jarman, my editor, is an erudite heroine – and to whom I am hugely indebted.

Dedication

This book is dedicated to Louise Reynolds, my darling mor, and Ralph Reynolds, my late father, who initiated me into the world of food and entertaining with unabashed dedication and passion. And to the fabulous Fleet family – Hilary, Mick, Nicky, Mel – and the remarkable Mrs O, Beryl Oborne, all of whom have been my right-hand 'men' through thick and thin during my catering career.

Preface

Starting and running a catering business is an aspiration many people have. Are you weighing up the pros and cons of this way of life? Are you keen to start a business from home and be your own boss, as well as entering a world of creativity and hospitality? You may also be contemplating a career change: many caterers come from a wide variety of backgrounds to fulfil their culinary dream.

Should I, could I, start my own catering service?

Outside catering is one of the fastest-growing businesses in the expanding food industry as more corporate companies realise how important it is to offer good food and service to guests and employees. Social (or private) caterers are also in a win-win situation thanks to a large number of people who have the disposable income to hire a caterer for entertaining at home, be it for a dinner party or a wedding in a marquee in their garden.

People increasingly want to eat freshly-prepared food to counteract the soulless fast food business, to eat food with real flavour made by a caterer with flair.

You can share in this growth market.

Why are people attracted to catering? In a study, over half questioned cited a desire to be independent in business, a third realising the potential within the catering industry. A strong urge to be your own employer is a powerful incentive. As we increasingly see our homes being used to their full potential, it is also seen as one of the best home businesses to start without having to resort to a dedicated outlet.

But what is catering? It is the business of preparing, presenting and serving hopefully simply sublime food appropriate to a brief. It is a key part of the hospitality industry, its growth quite phenomenal. But can it really be that simple? If so, why don't I just pack in the day job and get going – I'm a good cook. And I bet I know a few people who would just love to employ me. A cinch.

These first customers will pass on the good news to their friends and colleagues that they've found a reliable, enthusiastic, talented caterer. It's an ideal lifestyle change. It will be a fun venture and it'll make money from day one.

But you're not that naïve. This vital book will guide you through the steps needed to achieve a viable catering business.

I'll explain clearly and in depth everything you need to know about:

◆ how to approach prospective clients;
◆ how to price your services;
◆ how to define your style of food;
◆ what you need for premises including the kitchen and storage layout;
◆ menu composition;
◆ financing your business;
◆ the marketing of your company;
◆ how to run a safe, hygienic business;
◆ finding good staff and how to train them;
◆ customer relations;
◆ client invoicing;
◆ the day-to-day running of your venture.

I'll also tell you:

◆ what equipment to buy or hire;
◆ how to manage your store cupboard;
◆ how to deal with marquee companies, equipment hire companies, flower designers, musicians and others as part of your role in managing events.

This book will also, crucially, help you put yourself in your customers' shoes and guide you to building up a loyal trade. It is written for the small business caterer in mind, who wishes to start with minimal finance, basic equipment and become a successful small business caterer.

It is also invaluable for those already in the food business who wish to either expand or to trade up to meet current customer expectations – that is, offering more in the way of quality and style at all levels.

In reality, setting up a catering company is similar to any business. To someone who has had no contact or concept of the catering trade, it may appeal as a possible lucrative part- or full-time occupation.

But it takes a great deal of research, planning, commitment, hard work, some sleepless nights and a re-jigging of your life. You will be the employer, overseer, manager, leader, chef and chief bottle washer. Alternatively, you may wish to manage the business and take on a chef. Or vice versa.

What kind of a caterer do you see yourself as?

One who offers acceptable food and is in the business purely as a money-making venture? Or a caterer who sees the trade as a way of life and seeks to change, mature, explore new ideas and learn from others? But who also, through judicious management, stays afloat financially?

Your business will reflect your personality.

Being a caterer is a hard, unrelenting, competitive way of life but it can be hugely satisfying, rewarding, pleasurable, entertaining, intense and stimulating. The people you work with and become your customers are an immensely important factor in making this happen. You create an atmosphere for customers to relax in by offering good food thoughtfully and skilfully prepared, presented and served.

All human life is here, a veritable kaleidoscope of creativity and passion. And boundless energy, commitment and enthusiasm. Dispensing hospitality as well as terrific food and service is either the way of life you choose when running a catering business – or not. If not, is this the right business for you?

I have embraced a catering career for over twenty years as well as being a chef/restaurateur, restaurant critic and consultant, food journalist and author. I can assure you that the pure pleasure of pleasing clients is hard to beat if you have pulled out all the stops to create just what you promised to deliver – the best possible – and with care and attention to detail.

If you do decide to choose the life of a caterer, I wish you every possible success and fulfilment in one of the finer trades life has to offer – selling your culinary prowess (if you are indeed the chef) and management skills to an appreciative public.

1

Running Your Own Catering Business

As we've already established in the preface, running a catering business is a vision many people have. In reality, however, the thought is put on the back burner due to not being sure how to proceed.

WHY RUN A CATERING BUSINESS?

As an employee, your current work might be unrewarding, unstimulating and predictable, or you may be locked into a profession that no longer inspires. You long to develop a creative and business side you feel you have strengths in and being a caterer has an appeal for you.

Or you may be postponing the change as the leap from being an employee to self-employed and employer is a daunting one. But, having chosen this book, you are motivated to find out what the next steps are to becoming a caterer.

SKILLS YOU NEED

Before starting out, it is essential to consider whether you have what is needed to make a success of a business in catering.

- Are you a good organiser and planner?
- Are you a versatile cook?
- Are you a problem-solver?
- Are you able to delegate effectively?
- Will you be able to establish a good rapport with clients, staff and suppliers?
- Can you be hospitable towards guests when the party is in full swing?

Most of all: do you like people? If you find dealing with people on many levels a trial, then running a catering business might not be for you.

Examine what skills you possess, where you may have weaknesses and what you can do to overcome them. But, as you are considering this career move – or, indeed, career start – you may have what it takes.

When running a small catering business, you will need to be able to do almost everything from shopping, cooking, serving, delegating where possible, doing the bookkeeping, writing the quotes and confirmations, keeping up with hygiene rules and regulations and briefing staff, right down to the washing up. You will also continually need to market your brand-new career.

Skills such as the ability to manage in a crisis with a smile without losing your cool and to work with a number of different people, from parents of the bride to managing directors and flower designers, will all be put to the test in a catering environment.

◆ TIP ◆

It is essential to make sure there are no weaknesses in your business and that you have all the required skills and knowledge to pull it off successfully.

Catering, in its most basic form, is all about feeding people. This comes down to how efficient you are and how you are able to shape raw materials into interesting, distinctly tasty food. Meticulous planning is also a hugely important aspect of being a caterer, a skill which you will either learn or have already developed in another career or through running a household.

There will inevitably be a lot to learn as you start out in your new business. How to get guests to the table without the prepared food spoiling, and what kind of menus work for a variety of occasions are just a couple.

Once you get going, it's a good idea to review your first few events and see how you can improve on things like efficiency and organisation, the quantity and display of food, and instructions to staff.

You can ask yourself: Did you remember to take everything to the event? Did you anticipate the whole event or were there some surprises?

While you read this book and think about running a catering business, bear in mind that things won't be perfect from day one. Even several years down the line things always need improving. You will learn through trial and error as most new businesses do while you gain experience on a daily basis.

I'll come to list of what makes a good caterer later. First, what type of catering are you considering offering?

TYPES OF CATERING

Corporate catering

Winning a contract to be the sole caterer for a company is one way forward. You will be expected to offer whatever the company needs for the employees, from breakfasts, mid-morning coffees and snacks, lunches, afternoon teas and the occasional corporate reception on the premises.

Other corporate catering can include quoting for a specific occasion: a business lunch for overseas' guests, the Christmas party, the board of directors' all-day meeting, a long-serving member of staff's farewell party, a merger with another company resulting in a large reception, or the launch of a new product or service.

You could also be asked to quote for staff outings to sports, cultural or fundraising events, all increasingly important in the corporate calendar.

Much of the catering within large businesses is done in-house, but sometimes they ask for quotes from outside caterers for special occasions as they may be looking for better quality food and service that their own caterers can't provide. You could also consider doing lunches for a director's dining room.

Another way forward is to bid for a dedicated catering contract at a museum, an art gallery, stately homes open to the public, a garden centre, one of the many arts centres and theatres now gracing our cities or even an independent art house cinema.

Although you can approach a wide variety of places, larger establishments such as museums and theatres have a tendency to ask major catering companies to do the job. The contract with them is usually a long one which can't be broken without penalty.

◆ EXPERIENCE ◆

Theatre bosses were keen for me to take over their catering operation but the previous incumbents had locked the theatre into a lengthy contract. I could have offered fresh ingredients prepared and served imaginatively which would have reflected the creativity of the acclaimed theatre. Instead the public continued to be offered processed food of dubious quality.

If you do tender for such a contract and are lucky enough to be awarded it, it means a regular income but also less flexibility if you run a small company as you and your staff are tied to the company. Your company is responsible for the food, drink, staffing, equipment, health and hygiene, and on an agreed budget.

As your business grows and with it your staff, you may be able to handle more work – such as running an outlet supplying sandwiches and other fast, cold food to other businesses in the area and offering tailor-made catering to individual clients.

If you are keen to have weekends off, a contract within corporate catering would suit you. But be prepared to be flexible if asked to cater for a special occasion function as you need to safeguard your role as sole caterer for that company. Another caterer brought in might wow them with their food and service and challenge your place.

Social and specialised catering

This can be catering for private clients, or cooking on a semi-regular basis for a number of clients, for a fixed hourly fee, as well as running your private catering company. Events for both can include lunches, dinner parties, receptions, weddings, funerals, christenings, bar mitzvahs, birthday parties, barbecues and all manner of celebrations.

Apart from preparing the food from scratch (buying and starting some of the dishes at your premises and finishing them off at the client's), you will also be asked to provide, in most cases, the staff. For larger functions you will also be in charge of either providing the equipment (including linen, cutlery, plates and glassware) at a cost to the client or you will be asked to provide a list for the client so that they can arrange them for and they pay the hire company directly.

If you have amassed a good, reliable list of companies who can supply specialist categories, for larger parties you may wish to quote for all the types of drink required, the linen, table, chair and marquee hire, flowers and even musicians.

Many catering companies work in both corporate and specialised catering. When catering for a business reception, you might be approached by a guest to cater for a private event. They require different approaches as you will be dealing with very different people and situations. Corporate kitchens can vary enormously from just being somewhere to make morning coffee to, more rarely, a full-blown kitchen with all the whistles and bells. Private kitchens can be hell or heaven when it comes to space, (un)reliable ovens, roaming animals and just plain old-fashioned dirt.

◆ TIP ◆

Corporate businesses usually have a larger budget to work with, and social clients are more liable to try to cut costs when they become aware of the high costs of staffing, marquees, flowers and other expenses when planning a large function.

Other catering services

For those looking to give a less expensive catering service, cold service catering offers delivery of pre-packaged food including snacks (such as bagels, coffee and cakes), lunches, sandwiches, boxed food for corporate dos, trays of canapés and cold meats and cheeses. This convenience food is the important side of the business you offer rather than the service (other than being efficient, professional and punctual of course!).

Your food will be produced off-site rather than at the client's home or business and can be either bought-in ready-made food or made from scratch by your company.

Your cold service business might deliver to businesses, building sites, a client's home or even to a photo shoot (I have even been asked to cater for a private aircraft). Making sandwiches on a daily basis for a local store is also a possibility.

You may have an early morning start to get the food prepped and delivered, and the end of the day is usually late afternoon if you haven't been asked to cater for early evening business canapés. But, of course, there is the cleaning, shopping and invoicing to be taken care of during the day, which can stretch on to the evening.

If you choose to work in low-budget catering, there is a lot of competition that you will come up against. You will also be required to make a lot of food which will stifle your creativity; a high turnover is necessary for a viable business.

Working in the more expensive, classier end of catering is a lot more fun and creative, but client demands are high (as they should be). There is less competition but, when companies and individuals meet an economic slump, catering requirements can disappear overnight.

Whichever type of catering you feel is for you, don't bypass the opportunity of making your own produce, be it jam, conserves, sauces, cakes, biscuits, meringues or other items, to sell on to delicatessens, at farmers' markets (share a stall with an established stall holder to keep the costs down), farm shops and via your customers.

If you have a natural ability to teach cookery, or are a trained teacher in other subjects, offer yourself to adult education and catering colleges or teach cooking privately as well as running your business. At the start of your new venture, you will need all the regular income you can get.

WHAT NEXT?

Which type of catering appeals to you most? It's a good idea to work out what you can offer and put it down on paper. Define clearly your strengths, your vision, your possible target market. Look in the *Yellow Pages* and on the internet to see if the area is swamped by caterers or not.

Explore the market to see if you have struck lucky (is it a culinary desert out there?) and do some canvassing with businesses to find out their needs. Don't give up if you are competing against large caterers. They tend to offer mass-produced food. Your small operation would certainly be able to compete, either by price or offering better food and service.

If you see your catering business as a hobby or as purely a money-making venture, think again. It takes skill, dedication, hard work, long hours, an ability to sell your business to the public, enthusiasm and loads of energy and commitment. But, if you find the right market and are good at what you do, you will make a good living. And it is certainly never dull, especially working in the quality side of the business.

WORKING OUT YOUR STRENGTHS

First of all, examine your strengths and your character (if you are in partnership your colleagues should do it too) by asking yourself the questions that follow.

These questions need to be answered honestly. You may, of course, have never been tested in some areas. But you will need the majority of these qualities to run a successful business.

The concept of being your own boss is very energising but it is worth analysing your personality and those of others who are entering the business with you, both professionally and personally, to see if you – and they – have the necessary attributes.

This analytical list is not meant to put you off becoming a caterer but to help you become more aware of the skills it takes. If many of the answers are in your favour, other attributes will be achieved along the way.

- Are you fed up with your job and looking for a change of lifestyle?
- Do you want to be your own boss and keep the profits?
- Are you really positive about creating a new business?
- Are you motivated, organised and self-disciplined?
- Are you competitive?
- Are you efficient?
- Do you have a good grasp of how food is produced? (Not essential but it helps.)
- Have you taken on board the fact that you are saying goodbye to a secure pay packet and fringe benefits for the time being?
- Have you discussed with your family how this will affect them?
- As your busiest period could be weekends, how does this tally with family life?
- Are they committed to this change of lifestyle and back you wholeheartedly?
- Have you discussed with them the possibility of a lowering of standards of living until the business gets off the ground?
- Have you money to gamble, knowing you are taking a risk?
- Do you like people? Have you got the skills to deal with the idiosyncrasies of both customers and staff?
- Are you a good communicator?
- Are you prepared for perhaps a long haul before the business is successful?
- Do you and your business partner(s) share the right temperaments for the hospitality business?
- Are you a problem solver? A decision-maker?

- Are you confident enough to sell your business plan to banks, customers and the media?
- Can you take advice? Learn new skills?
- Can you delegate?
- Can you prioritise?
- How good at stress are you?
- Do you have good health?
- Do you have a warm personality? A hospitable nature?
- Do you have the physical and emotional stamina to work long hours?
- Are you flexible? Calm? Reasonable? Positive?
- How do you really feel about the service industry?
- Is your goal realistic and attainable?

Don't be put off by this lengthy list. Not all of the questions may apply to you as you may have partners, colleagues and staff who may be able to fulfil some of the roles required for running a successful catering company.

2

Getting into the Catering Business

It may be that you have been working in catering as an employee for a time and would like to open your own business. Or perhaps you have always wanted to be in the food industry, with catering at the front of the aspirational list. You could, of course, be starting out from a totally different non-catering direction, but with a passion for food, as well as wanting to be your own boss.

Whatever your background, you'll need to consider what your first step to get into the business will be. There are four tried and tested ways to become a caterer:

1. Starting your own business from scratch and developing it slowly but surely.

2. Buying an existing business with premises, equipment, staff, a client base and a good name and reputation.

3. Becoming an investment/working partner in an existing business.

4. Working for a catering company to learn the business with well-respected professionals with a view to becoming a partner.

STARTING YOUR OWN BUSINESS FROM SCRATCH

◆ EXPERIENCE ◆

Peter Gladwin, chef/owner of Party Ingredients whose offices and kitchens face the Thames in London, was one such beginner. He now employs 140 in his catering operation and his four London-based restaurants, and he started catering from his small flat in Battersea, London 30 years ago.

'I just felt I could do better in the trade. There were grumpy little old ladies in black pinnies at the parties we went to and when we [friends and staff] started Party Ingredients, we introduced a customer-focused service with younger people serving. Of course it was hit and miss and we did everything from taking jobs in London to going all over the country. We just mucked in together.'

Many small caterers have started from scratch. Peter's experience is very much in keeping with those who start from nothing. You may decide to open your own business after several successes organising and cooking for large functions for family, friends or fundraising events. Or you may have worked in catering and decide you can do better, as in Peter's case.

Party Ingredients has risen to cater for the Queen Mother's 100th birthday celebrations at the City of London's Guildhall, 10 Downing Street, state banquets, weddings, charity events and private parties. Peter is very much a hands-on employer who cooks at one of his restaurants as well as running the business.

Most caterers start part time from their kitchens on a very small scale. There are, however, lots of things to prepare. For example, you will need ample refrigeration and separate storage space amongst other things. You will have to check with your local environmental health officer who will need to inspect your kitchen for health and safety reasons, and you must register your premises with the environmental health service at your local authority at least 28 days before opening. You must get liability insurance too as you could to be sued if food poisoning or an accident occurs.

There is more information on the dos and don'ts and must-haves as set down by the Food Safety Agency in Chapter 4.

The growth of the small caterer is by word of mouth but marketing is of vital importance too. Gone are the days when you could just hope for client referral to make a decent living in anything, including catering. See Chapter 6 for lots of information about marketing.

Going down this home route has many advantages: it keeps overheads to a minimum, works around family life, and still, hopefully, gives you time for your own interests. You will be able to assess if this is the business for you after a period of time. If not, just pull out gracefully with little investment and expense apart from perhaps bruised pride.

You may decide you like cooking and serving food professionally, organising the party, and enjoy the interaction with clients. If you find that you are in demand and that your stamina and family aren't suffering, you could be on to a winning career.

◆ EXPERIENCE ◆

Ursula Crocker, from West Sussex, started Cook & Buttle 13 years ago with Nigel Chandler, her business partner. She and Nigel worked together in a ducal household; Ursula the cook, Nigel the butler, hence the name. They cater for private dinner parties, weddings and other events.

Ursula returned to Britain from Brazil after years of running restaurants with her husband, Chris. She decided to continue cooking from home as she had three children. 'Cooking was something I could do easily,' she says.

She advertised in the parish magazine and, by word of mouth ('it wasn't an overnight success'). Ursula now has a dedicated kitchen in a converted dairy. She sensibly involved the Environmental Health inspectors from the start so that she didn't have any costly mistakes by contravening any laws.

> ◆ **EXPERIENCE** *continued* ◆
>
> She believes her success has been founded on a personal touch and being consci-
> entious. 'We did it with no money,' she says, 'and we had no capital tied up in
> equipment or vans.' There are no overheads (the dairy is part of Ursula's family
> home) and therefore even more profitable.
>
> The quotes and menus were initially written by hand. Nigel looks after the
> accounts, the organisation of staff and is in charge of the running of the event and
> Ursula is in charge of the menus, quotes, letters of confirmation, shopping, cooking
> and presentation.

MAKING YOUR BUSINESS UNIQUE

Of course, home catering covers all sorts of food preparation. If, for example, your forte is cake-making, you could market it well. But does it have a
unique selling point? It has to stand out from the crowded cake market to
be a success.

This applies to any product. It must be good enough to give you a reasonable profit margin, taking into account all your other costs such as your
ingredients, packaging, overheads (lighting, gas, electricity, phone calls,
labelling, cleaning materials, petrol). And don't forget to factor in your
own, very precious, time too.

Take a leaf out of Ursula's book. She decided to branch out by selling
ready-made meals at farmers' markets, making home-made terrines, pates,
dips and other specialities using local produce. Keeping up with trends and
reinventing a business is an excellent way to keep it fresh, alive and exciting.
Find your own unique selling point to make the grade. Look at what is happening locally or nationally and adapt the best ideas to suit your business.

BEING A SOLE/JOINT PARTNER

The definition of a sole trader is that the business is owned and operated
by one person. If two people join forces it is known as a partnership. A sole
trader, whether or not in a partnership, is personally liable for debts.

Advantages

◆ A sole or joint partnership business is easier to set up with less formality and legal constraints than a partnership or company.
◆ There is no need to share the profits with anyone other than your agreed partner(s).
◆ A sole partner has complete control over the business, the direction it is heading, the style of the food, expenditure on marketing etc.
◆ There is no one to answer to as there would be if in a partnership or company.

Disadvantages

◆ If not in a partnership, you are the only boss and, as such, can find it difficult to get away at all, let alone to have a holiday.
◆ You are responsible for all the paperwork.
◆ You are responsible for liability and business debts.
◆ You don't share other people's expertise, fresh ideas and experience, thereby perhaps limiting your business.
◆ It can be lonely running your own business.

PARTNERSHIPS

You may be working with an active partner, one who is involved on a daily basis; a dormant partner who is a financial backer; or a silent one offering a name which lends some weight to the business.

If you are entering the business with a partner or partners, there is a strong case for setting up a partnership agreement in conjunction with a lawyer.

Some points to consider:

◆ The name, location and purpose of the partnership.
◆ What each partner brings financially to the business.
◆ What strengths each partner contributes to the business.
◆ What equipment each partner contributes to the business.
◆ A detailed outline regarding business expenses and how to handle them.
◆ What each partner is responsible for in detail.

◆ What each partner will receive for a salary.

◆ How the profits and losses are to be distributed to partners.

◆ How accounts will be handled.

◆ How the partnership can be modified or terminated.

◆ TIP ◆

In a partnership, all partners are jointly liable for debts. If you come up against a legal problem you will be risking your personal assets.

FORMING A COMPANY

The same principles apply to forming a company as a partnership (see above). The company is the business and directors are the shareholders. A limited company means that the company, not the individual directors, is liable for any debts.

If forming a company, do shop around for a solicitor's package deal. If you decide to operate as a company, you will have to pay corporation tax and make company tax returns. Soon after the end of the accounting period the Inland Revenue will send you a notice asking you to make a company tax return.

◆ TIP ◆

Your local Enterprise Agency (www.enterprise-centre.co.uk or info@enterprise-centre.co.uk) can explain in full the advantages and disadvantages of being a sole trader or forming a company.

Company tax

If you decide to operate as a company, you will have to pay corporation tax and make company tax returns. Soon after the end of the accounting period the Inland Revenue will send you a notice asking you to make a company tax return.

Before setting up a company, consult an accountant regarding corporation tax. Unlike a sole trader or a partnership, company tax needs to be audited, which is an added expense.

You must normally pay any tax due by nine months and one day after the end of the accounting period. If, at that stage, you have not yet completed your company tax return you must make an estimate of what you think is due and pay that.

Send a completed tax return, including your accounts and tax computations, to the Inland Revenue by the filing date (which usually 12 months after the end of the accounting period). If the return is not delivered by this date, a penalty will occur.

Speak to your accountant or tax advisor to decide on the accounting period and tell your tax office. Work out the dates by which you need to pay tax and make your company tax return.

Plan ahead to make sure that accounts and tax computations are prepared in good time but always communicate with your tax office if you fall behind. Make sure it's a two-way dialogue for peace of mind.

Keep proper business records (see Chapter 5: Business Finances) and keep these for six years after the end of the accounting period.

BUYING AN EXISTING BUSINESS

It may seem like an easy option to buy an existing business, which is ready-made with staff, client list, premises, equipment, a good name and reputation. But first, decide if you:

◆ have enough funding to buy the business and run it for several months until you get established. Think about how much you will need.
◆ have sufficient catering experience to take over the business. This should cover your culinary strengths, your business backbone and financial ability.
◆ have appropriate, catering experience: you must be able to match the existing clients' needs and ensure you can deliver the goods, particularly if the business you are taking over is more upmarket.
◆ are physically and mentally able to work a very long day: 14–16 hours is an average. Remember that it will even out once you are fully in charge and have gained the trust of your client base and established your business pattern.

Finding an existing business to buy

This tends to be a buyers' market. Catering businesses can have a burnout rate due to the owners working long hours over a period of years. This is especially true if owned by a sole caterer who is keen to retire.

Ways to proceed:

◆ Look at existing businesses for sale in catering magazines such as *Caterer and Hotelkeeper*, or in your local papers in the 'businesses for sale' section.
◆ Contact agencies that advertise in these publications to find out what is on their books or to express an interest in buying a business.
◆ Contact caterers directly. They may be keen to sell.

◆ TIP ◆

Buy a deli or restaurant for its premises if you can get a good deal. Either keep the business going while running a catering company or close it down and use the premises as a catering company. If you keep the restaurant or deli going you get double service from your premises. Having premises gives you prestige and an extra marketing tool because you are visible.

Top tips for buying a business

◆ **Make absolutely sure that it has good records and bookkeeping.** You must know the annual turnover and profit for at least the past three years to be able to determine if the business is viable and that you are making a sound purchase.
◆ **Always use a solicitor and an accountant.** The accountant will help you determine a fair price. He or she will be aware of sharp practices and if the bookkeeping has been done professionally or not.
◆ **Be aware that the seller may augment figures** to make the gross annual profit and net profits look very high. Obviously, if these are both high then the business looks very successful and therefore a good bet. But is it?
◆ **Discuss the client list with the seller in depth.** Examine the list carefully. What kind of catering does the company offer? How often does each client feature? Is there good repeat business?

- **Discuss the staff with the seller.** How many staff are employed/semi-employed? What is the rate of pay, travel expenses, the package offered to staff (e.g. pension, sickness benefit)?
- **Look at the profit margins.** What are the profit margins per event? Is the caterer giving value for money or supplying quantity instead of quality? Are there any outstanding debts with suppliers? What is the geographical business radius?
- **Establish what kind of a reputation the company has.** If it's less than your standards, or has a less than impressive record, then it might be an uphill struggle to convince people that you offer an improved service and better food. Look at the business with fine toothcomb.
- **Offer to work alongside the owner** for a week or so to find out more about the business. You will then know if it is for you or not. The owner should be very happy to oblige. If not, what are they hiding?
- **Don't accept the asking price of the business.** It is time to bargain. You should take into consideration the state of the kitchens (do they need an overhaul or are they pristine?), the age of the equipment, the number of clients, and the turnover. Use your lawyer for the actual negotiations, but make sure you are involved at all levels of the transactions.

And, before signing the agreement:

- **Ask the seller for a thorough inventory** of the kitchen and hire equipment such as pots and pans, cookers, refrigeration, glass, cutlery, linen and plates, office furniture and computing equipment, any van or lorry vehicles or other items.
- **Make sure that the seller passes you a list of clients** with all the relevant details including who to contact and how (email addresses, phone numbers, when and what the last catering event was for the client, for example). This is known as goodwill, and also includes the name of the business and all that is part of a viable business.
- **Make sure that there is a covenant** within the agreement that the seller will not compete within a designated area and not for a minimum period to be agreed on. If you don't do this, more unscrupulous sellers may just carry on with their existing customers, leaving you an empty shell of a business so insist on a covenant.

Of course, you won't take over exactly where the seller left off. The business will change once you have taken over. That is guaranteed. Some clients won't like your style of food or service perhaps and may wish to find another caterer. Conversely, they may be bowled over by your excellent standards and presentation, your efficiency and professionalism. You may have to convince those on the client list to try your new style and if they are reluctant to, discuss their needs with them. Asking them to sample dishes from your menu to convince them of your skills is one way forward.

BECOMING A PARTNER IN AN EXISTING BUSINESS

If you have worked in catering and have gained excellent experience and skills along the way, you may wish to move up the business ladder and work alongside a partner in an existing business. (See Chapter 5 for more information.)

It goes without saying that any agreement you enter into with a partner must be documented in full and be legally binding. You will need to find a lawyer who deals in partnership law. They will advise you on what you need to do and what costs are involved in setting up a partnership.

There are different kinds of partnerships. You may wish to join a friend, colleague, acquaintance or complete stranger who has a business and is looking for expansion.

Before you commit to partnership, think through the following:

◆ You should have the same aims and aspirations as your partner.
◆ You should have the same standards, attention to detail and work ethic.
◆ If there might be clashes regarding issues such as the menu, presentation, treatment of clients and staff, discuss them at length to come to a uniform conclusion.
◆ Look at the different strengths you and your partner(s) can offer the business so that it is a stronger company. Perhaps you have a good grasp of accountancy, and your prospective partner is strong in marketing.
◆ All partners should take on equal responsibilities if you are equal partners. Make sure you spell out the responsibilities and percentage of the profits of each partner.

◆ If you are a junior partner (one who has less experience and doesn't put in the same amount of money) with less than half the ownership, have each partners' work description written up or you may end up with a lot more of the dogsbody, menial work.

◆ Make sure that you have a list of all the contributions each person makes to the partnership. For example, who put up the cash, who owns the property, what equipment belongs to which partner. Draw up an agreement with a solicitor.

◆ TIP ◆

The agreement should contain provisions for buying the other partner out, should this arise, and what happens if one partner dies.

The advantages of a partnership are manifold and include the possibility of taking a holiday without closing the business for a week or two and sharing the strengths of each partner.

WORKING FOR A CATERING COMPANY TO LEARN THE ROPES

If you have little or no knowledge of the catering business but you are a good cook with some of strengths listed in Chapter 1, working for a respected catering company could be a fast way for you to learn the ropes.

Choose your catering company carefully before approaching them to see if there is a suitable vacancy. But if you have chosen the wrong company who you feel doesn't mirror your wishes or standards, exit the door and do some research before becoming employed by another one.

WHICH ROUTE TO TAKE?

Choosing which catering route to take may seem daunting at first, and if you are still undecided, talk to established caterers to find out more information. If you don't know any personally, I suggest you find one (but not in your area!) via the *Yellow Pages* or the internet and call or email them. If calling, do ask if it is a convenient time to speak to them as they may be up to their elbows in couscous. Dedication, research and perseverance is all in any enterprise.

3

Finding and Equipping Your Business Premises

This chapter moves you to the next stage: your business premises, be they at home or on dedicated premises. Running a safe, hygienic business is one of the biggest tests a caterer has to deal with. This chapter covers:

◆ food handling on and off your premises;
◆ adhering to hygiene standards and Environmental Health requirements;
◆ Food Safety Act and Food Premises' Regulations;
◆ temperature controls;
◆ types of food poisoning;
◆ finding and registering food premises;

◆ property conversion, planning applications and dealing with architects;
◆ design and construction for kitchens;
◆ lighting and structural requirements;
◆ storage;
◆ equipment needed in a dedicated kitchen;
◆ ventilation;
◆ refuse and drainage;
◆ pest control.

The amount of regulations you must adhere to will depend on whether you run a small business from home, or have dedicated premises. The bigger the company and staff, the more rules and regulations will come into play.

Do contact your local environmental health officers about required standards for running a catering business. This should be done when you are looking at premises to get a clear picture of the requirements. Some properties may not be at all suitable or may not be able to be changed to fit the required standards. You will also need to discuss the requirements for the use of your home as your kitchen may not pass the test. Free advice is gladly given.

REGISTERING FOOD PREMISES

If you are planning to start a new catering business, you must register your premises with the environmental health service at your local authority. Registration of premises used for a food business including market stalls, delivery vehicles and other moveable structures is required by law.

Time limit

You must register your business at least 28 days before opening a new food business. If you run a food business for more than five days in any five consecutive weeks, you must tell the local authority about any premises you use for storing, selling, distributing or preparing food. Contact your local authority for the appropriate (and very straightforward) form. There is no charge.

Who has to register

Most types of food businesses must be registered including those run from home, mobile premises, stalls and burger vans. If in doubt, ask whether your business must be registered. This also applies to those using the same food premises such as village halls or conference centres. Ask the person responsible for these premises if they are registered if you are catering at these places. In short, if you use your own premises for catering as well as catering in another food premises, both must be registered. If the premises are used only occasionally such as a village hall, the law also allows some flexibility. But all premises still need to be registered.

MOVEABLE/TEMPORARY PREMISES

If you run a food business from mobile or temporary premises, you need to know about the same hygiene issues as other food businesses. However, as space is limited, the legal requirements are slightly different and allow greater flexibility.

Moveable/temporary premises used for the occasional catering purpose including marquees, market stalls and mobile sales vehicles have different requirements to that of a permanent structure. You must make sure:

- premises and vending machines are kept in good repair and kept clean to avoid contaminating food and harbouring pests. They must also be well sited, designed and constructed;
- there are appropriate facilities to maintain adequate personal hygiene;
- surfaces are easily cleanable;
- there is provision for the cleaning of equipment and utensils, and food;
- there is adequate provision of hot and cold water;
- there is adequate storage and waste disposal;
- there are adequate facilities for monitoring suitable temperature and conditions for keeping food at the right temperature;
- food is placed where there is no risk of contamination.

Once you have registered with the local authority you need to notify them of the change of proprietor if the business changes or if there is a change of address at which moveable premises are kept. The new proprietor will have to complete an application form.

◆ **TIP** ◆

Don't forget to register as self-employed with the tax office.

WORKING FROM OR AT HOME

This can be a great way to save money, but there are some special rules for those who use their home as a workplace.

◆ **Check with your mortgage lender or landlord** before you start your business as mortgage or tenancy agreements may prevent you from running a business from home.
◆ **Check with your insurers** to make sure you are adequately covered for running a business from home.
◆ **If your business results in a marked increase in traffic** or people calling in a residential area this may have an impact on the surrounding area and you will need to apply for planning permission.
◆ **If your business disturbs your neighbours** with extra noise or smell you will have to apply for planning permission from your local authority.
◆ **Your local council may charge business rates** for the part of your property you use for work but it depends on the circumstances of each case. (Check with your local branch of the Valuation Office Agency for advice by contacting them on 020 7506 1700 or www.voa.gov.uk)
◆ **If you want to change the way premises are used,** you may need to obtain planning permission from your local authority. Any significant building work must comply with building regulations.

RENTING OR BUYING DEDICATED CATERING PREMISES

If it is not appropriate or possible for you to base your business at home – you may not have enough facilities or simply want to keep home and work separate – you will probably consider renting or buying premises.

If this is the case, here are some tips:

◆ Get a solicitor who specialises in commercial property transactions for either renting or buying a property.
◆ Have a business plan that has been approved by a bank.

- Go through the *Yellow Pages* and local papers or buy a catering magazine such as *Caterer and Hotelkeeper* to see which estate agents to contact.
- Good agents will get to know you, the client, instead of introducing you to masses of properties that don't suit your wishes. What kind of property are you seeking? Make sure you get this across when talking to an agent, but be prepared to be flexible when viewing properties as you may surprise yourself.
- First and foremost you must have an excellent understanding of your market. This comes first before entering into any contract despite the excitement of falling in love with a property. Do you fit into this area? Who will your customers be? Look at the marketing chapter for more advice on how to gauge your market and the possibilities that exist for expanding your business.

If you decide to rent:

- Measure the property yourself, as the area given by estate agents or landlord can sometimes be more, and the rent therefore could be lowered.
- Negotiate a lower rent if taking out a long lease.
- If the property needs repairs or major re-decoration, ask for a rent-free period or discount until these are carried out.
- Always get an agreement in writing for all dealings with landlords or estate agents especially for any major alterations you would like to make to the property.
- Check on planning permission with your local council if putting up new signage or changing use of a property.

Leases: a brief guide
If you do decide to rent premises, this useful information will help you.

The average leasehold lease is 25 years, although some other leases are 20 or 15 years. Other leases can be negotiated with the landlord. A freehold lease's finance changes only with the cost of borrowing.

Landlords are looking for long-term investments and if the tenant has no track record, the landlord may ask for a rent deposit of a year in advance or a bank guarantee. However, the tenant may ask for a rent-free period if money is being spent on the property such as re-wiring, re-decorating or new plumbing. Ask a tax advisor about setting off a large rent deposit against taxes as the period of non-profit making needs to be taken into account.

If the lease is a full repairing and insuring one with five-year rent reviews, the rent only increases, never decreases. A full repairing and insuring lease means that you are liable for all repairs to the property as well as insuring it. A smart move would be to first employ a solicitor, have a survey and ensure, if the property needs some attention, to have a schedule of works drawn up by the owner before taking over the premises. As it is quite a complicated area, do consult a solicitor.

The amount of rent increase can be calculated on profits or a comparable method of calculation.

A break clause is advisable. This is a walk-away sum should the lease be broken. A sub-let clause should also be included.

The shorter the lease, the less security there is for the business and its borrowing power. A longer lease could be used as security against a loan as well as a psychological feeling of security.

From viewing to signing via legalities and licensing your property can vary from eight to 12 weeks depending on the complexities of the property and the availability of your finances. It can also be affected by your council's efficiency. Change of use can take one month.

◆ TIP ◆

Always get professional advice with a lease, and get the rent right. This is key to any successful business.

Buying a property

You may wish to buy a property for your business as that way you can alter the premises to suit you, which would not be possible if you rented.

(Alterations are, of course, subject to planning approval if the structure requires much alteration.) It is also easier to sell a business if you own the property and it is a good investment. Buying a business property follows the same principles as buying a house.

Some tips:

◆ Find an architect whose practice deals in the catering industry to visit the property with you to discuss any alterations you may want to make. Be guided by his or her expertise.
◆ Check on planning permission with the your local council in relation to change of use, signage, and access to property via new doors for example.
◆ Instruct a solicitor to act for you.
◆ Communication is vital between buyer and seller. Keep people up to speed.
◆ Discuss with environmental health officers basic requirements such as hand basins for staff, refrigeration, kitchen extractors, fire extinguishers etc.

RENTING OR BUYING AN ESTABLISHED CATERING COMPANY

Taking on an established catering company is a quicker entry into the business as it has a ready-made client base as well as equipment, staff and suppliers. But do look at businesses you visit with a fine toothcomb.

Here are some points to consider when looking at an established company.

◆ Are the owners experiencing catering fatigue or are there other reasons such as retirement/illness for the sale/change of lease?
◆ Is there area development which will adversely affect the area? Or, conversely, add to the customer potential?
◆ How old is the business and how many years has it been profitable?
◆ What is the profit margin for the past few years?
◆ What percentage of repeat business is there?
◆ Do the books look accurate? Do the assets outweigh the liabilities? Ask your solicitor's or bank manager's advice.
◆ Have all renovations been undertaken with the necessary approval?

Local government and your business

You need to establish a relationship with your local authority for planning permission, building regulations and any structural changes you wish to make to the property. Are you converting a property? Custom-building one? It is vital to get their advice and/or permission before embarking on any building.

- If converting a property, get approval for change of use permission. Consider consulting a professional to sort out the paperwork if the process is complicated. (It will help your sanity!)
- If you wish to lodge a complaint against your local authority because you feel the handling of your application was badly undertaken, contact the authority first then, if still dissatisfied, contact a higher authority. You may wish to discuss possible steps with your solicitor or a professional planning consultant.
- If you decide to alter your premises to house your business, you may need planning permission and you will also need to pay business rates. Contact your local authority for information. Planning application forms are available from your local council together with guidance notes. Unless your application is simple, it is advisable to discuss it with your planning officer first.

There are three types of application:

1. **Outline planning application**
   If you are proposing to put up a building, you can make an outline application to find out whether permission will be given in principle.

2. **Application for approval of reserved matters**
   After receiving outline planning permission you must seek approval in detail. If your new proposals are in any way different, you must make a full planning application (see the next step).

3. **Application for full planning permission**
   This is the route to take if you want to change the use of a property or if you want to build but not to follow the approach outlined in the first two steps.

SCRUTINISING THE PROPERTY

Get a surveyor to help you before you rent or buy, just as you would do for buying a house. Scrutinising a rented property too is vital as the lease could be a long one and, if you enter into a full repairing lease, it could cost you dearly if you don't establish at the beginning of the negotiations any problems with the building.

Therefore, view properties very carefully. It will help you negotiate your price if you have a sound checklist and a list of items to discuss with builders for quotations.

Take into account the following:

- Are there cracks or any visible structural problems?
- Are the ceilings flaking? Any damp patches?
- Is the flooring, particularly in the kitchen areas, suitable and in good condition?
- Is there good drainage?
- Does the flooring slope; have holes; is it uneven; are there changes of floor level?
- Are kitchen surfaces and equipment surfaces in sound condition?
- Is there adequate lighting or does new lighting have to be installed?
- Do stairs have hand rails?
- Are windows in good order? Check for rotting wood.
- Is the roof sound?
- Does the whole property need to be redecorated?
- Is there good ventilation?
- Is there an adequate supply of hot water and drinking water?
- Is appropriate fire safety installed?
- If equipment such as fridges and cookers are included in the deal, are they moveable to clean behind, in good working order, well maintained and clean?

VENTILATION REQUIREMENTS

Good ventilation provides a comfortable working environment, reduces humidity, removes contaminated greasy air, steam and cooking smells. It also prevents condensation which will ultimately mean less redecoration and maintenance.

Cost cutting – if you don't put in the appropriate ventilation suitable to your business – can result in high temperatures and humidity with increased risk of food poisoning due to increased heat and condensation. Remember to keep ventilation maintained so it remains effective. External ducts require planning permission in most cases and need to be positioned carefully to avoid fallout with neighbours.

There are three main types of ventilation:

◆ **Natural ventilation:** only suitable for small scale operations, this system is seldom ideal as it relies on open windows and doors, is subject to the weather and is least effective in hot weather. Mesh screening is necessary to keep out flying insects.
◆ **Extract only system:** a simple, inexpensive technique which uses an extractor fan to draw out hot or stale air, cooking fumes and steam. Useful to ensure that cooking smells are prevented from spreading to other rooms.
◆ **Combined extract/inlet system:** the most efficient system with the fullest control, it balances the flow of air in and out of the area. The design is based on a combination of ducting and fan exhausting the hot, damp and sometimes greasy air from the area with controllable replacement fresh air.

HYGIENE

Hygiene is of the utmost importance in your catering business. It is vital to have an adequate water supply, wash basins, sinks, washing-up equipment and good drainage so that you run a safe business. Your environmental health officer is only too happy to give (free) advice on these matters to safeguard the public.

Water supply and drainage

When renting or buying a property, make sure that these points are covered with the buyer/landlord and with your staff. Water is something we take for granted and it is vital that you get this right for a safe, hygienic business.

- Drinkable (also known as potable) water must be used to ensure food is not contaminated.
- Only drinkable water can be used to make ice cubes.
- Water from a storage tank or private water supply should be monitored on a regular basis.
- In new premises, drinking water installation should be disinfected. Your local authority or architect can advise you on what to do.
- Drainage facilities must be designed and constructed to avoid the risk of contamination of foodstuffs.
- All sink, wash basin and dishwasher pipes should discharge directly into the drainage system through a trapped gully to prevent foul odours.
- As this is a complex area with floor channels, deep seal gullies and sewers do contact your local authority for further information.

Sinks and washing equipment

You will need adequate facilities for food preparation, staff use, crockery, general cleaning and disinfecting of work tools and equipment. All these require a supply of hot and cold water, should be able to be cleaned easily and should be well sited. Below are some recommendations, but take advice from your environmental health officer, particularly if you have small premises with little space.

Position hand dryers carefully so that dirt and bacteria aren't blown around food areas. As they are slow and inefficient and perhaps put people off frequent hand washing, disposable towels are your best bet.

Sinks for washing food must be separate from hand washing sinks; separate hand wash basins are recommended to be placed in each work and food service area including the bar and preferably at the entrance of the kitchen. Stainless steel wash basins are strongly recommended but glazed ceramic basins are acceptable. Domestic sinks are not acceptable. Wash basins with foot, knee, 'automatic operated' taps or mixer taps are deemed a good idea but are not necessary.

> **◆ TIP ◆**
>
> Lavatories must not be next to food handling space. Hand-washing facilities must be provided with hot and cold water and materials for cleaning hands.

Commercial quality stainless steel sinks, one or more, are recommended for the main sinks with one or more deep sinks for pot washing. In large catering premises separate sinks are required for each of the following: vegetables, salads, meat and fish. A separate sink for mops, buckets etc should be located outside the food area.

A dishwashing machine with a fitted water softener (for certain hard water areas) is recommended for all but the smallest of food premises. A double sink with double stainless steel (never wooden) drainer is also recommended and may be used instead of a dishwasher but why be hard on yourself? Commercial dishwashers take very little time in comparison to domestic dishwashers to operate and are designed with a simple interior and simple controls.

Refuse storage

It is important to be able to dispose of refuse safely while it is on your premises and before it is taken away so that is doesn't attract vermin and flying insects which can lead to infection, contamination and food poisoning. Most of it is just basic, good common sense.

Don't allow food waste and other refuse to accumulate in food rooms. Waste must be in closed, sound, easy-to-clean containers.

Free-standing or wall-mounted lidded holders for plastic bags should be provided or a foot operated plastic lidded bin lined by a plastic bag. Remove full bags and clean containers and surrounding area frequently.

Refuse storage and removal must be arranged and designed to be protected from pests (those pesky flying insects plus cats, dogs and foxes in particular) and mustn't contaminate premises, drinking water or equipment. Either site bins externally with a roofed shield if space allows or in a non food area with plenty of ventilation.

Keep wheelie bins clean and clearly marked with the catering company's name and street number if applicable.

Bulk collection of refuse can be arranged for larger businesses. Contact your local authority for what is on offer as the type of service offered varies as well as charges. Contact them too for disposal of white goods (fridges and freezers for example).

Pest control

Keeping infestations of rodents, insects or other food pests out of your premises is a priority. They will be attracted to food sitting on counters, in open bins, bags of waste which have accumulated, dirty surfaces and on floors. It is forbidden to store food on floors – it must be kept on shelving.

Any infestation will lead to contamination of food and food surfaces, damage of food stocks and the building. To combat this, maintain high standards of cleanliness, good housekeeping and food storage.

Both country and town have vermin problems with cockroaches, mice, pharaoh ants (tiny brown ants) and rats, all of which can be dealt with by local authority or private contractor exterminators. The cleaner your premises (and that means behind fridges etc where vermin love to congregate), the fewer problems you'll encounter.

Food preparation areas and storage areas

Floors, walls and ceilings in contact with food must be in a sound condition and easy to clean. They should be smooth, hard-wearing, washable and in a good state of repair.

Ceilings must be designed and constructed in a way that prevents condensation, build-up of dirt, moulds and shedding of particles (paint or building materials that could contaminate food, for example).

Windows and other openings (you may have a door leading from the kitchen to the outside) must be designed and built in a way that prevents dirt building up. You may also be asked to fit insect-proof screens by your local authority. Doors must also be easy to clean.

All equipment that comes into contact with food must be in good repair and be easily cleanable.

♦ TIP ♦

You must provide adequate cleaning and disinfecting tools, utensils and equipment and keep them apart from food storage.

THE KITCHEN

Layout of the kitchen

To provide a safe working environment and to avoid cross contamination of food at all stages the design of your kitchen and storage areas is of great importance. Your layout should be built around the operation and not the other way around.

Remember:

♦ A smaller kitchen operation will have to compromise on space.
♦ What's important is not how much a kitchen costs but what you do with the space.
♦ An older building, such as a 17th century cottage, may not have the perfect layout. Take this into consideration when looking at properties and decide if the areas can be made to work – or not. Can staff carry work out safely?

A logical flow of operation of delivery, storage, prepping, cooking, packing, disposal of waste, rubbish storage and collection with as many clearly designated areas for each stage of work is necessary to avoid cross contamination.

For example, a box is delivered and is put down on the counter where chicken is being prepared. Not only can the box have dirt on the bottom but it may now have picked up raw chicken bits. That box may be moved to another part of the kitchen and the cross contamination is now in its second stage.

The kitchen counter may also be contaminated from dirt on the box; perhaps it was put down on the pavement before being taken into the restaurant.

All of this can be avoided if a logical flow – and common sense – is adhered to. Think about the following:

◆ Is space limited so that efficiency is impaired?
◆ Is cleaning difficult?
◆ Is there sufficient space so that when your staff are working at benches (counters to you and me) and other fixed equipment, other people can pass? Remember too that the layout of cookers, ovens, fryers, refrigeration and other hot machinery must be taken into account to avoid congestion.

Think about what you expect the kitchen to achieve. What kind of food will you be offering to clients? This will dictate what kind of equipment you need and where it should be placed for efficiency and practicality. What can the kitchen handle?

If you are planning to make a lot of sandwiches for an outlet, for example, you will need a good amount of counter space to place boards, breads, bowls, fillings, wrapping, and labels. You may need less space if you are catering for small parties but always think big when calculating your countertop preparation area.

◆ TIP ◆

If you are working from dedicated premises, the hub of your catering premises has to work efficiently. Your business can fail on the basis of a poorly-designed kitchen.

Storage

If you require space for a lot of kitchen equipment – electrical goods, a good variety of pots and pans, bowls etc – you will need copious amounts of shelving. But if you are not supplying your customers with plates, glasses, cutlery and other dining equipment but hiring them, you may not need as much space.

Ask a commercial kitchen equipment company for their advice. You may be taking over a premises that already has some equipment and only need to add other equipment to upgrade the kitchen.

Or you may be starting from scratch. Do involve the chef (if it isn't you), partners in the business, the builder, plumber, carpenter and architect in these crucial discussions, be it an upgrade or a whole new kitchen.

A catering kitchen is divided into prepping area/cooking area, washing up area and service. Storage takes place in all four areas. A smaller kitchen operation may have to compromise on space while larger kitchens will have the following prepping areas to function at speed: vegetables, fish, poultry, meat, desserts.

You will need storage areas for the following:

◆ vegetable and fruit produce (away from heat);
◆ dry goods (away from heat);
◆ linen;
◆ staff belongings;
◆ cleaning materials, buckets, mops, light bulbs, toilet paper, refuse bags;
◆ alcohol;
◆ rubbish;
◆ paperwork. Don't underestimate the amount of paperwork! If no space is available try to find a permanent spot to store it.

KITCHEN EQUIPMENT

Consult the *Yellow Pages* for catering companies that supply the large equipment, pots, pans, clothing and knives. Your library will have London and other large town's *Yellow Pages* (or look on the internet) for details of large specialist companies. Or ask a respected caterer or two for personal recommendations.

My recommendations for basic kitchen requirements for a dedicated kitchen are the following:

◆ double oven with four or six gas burners;
◆ grill or salamander (high level grill);
◆ deep-fat fryer;
◆ large commercial fridge or walk-in fridge;

- freezer;
- double sink;
- hand basin;
- sink (near the cooking area preferably);
- washing-up area with commercial dishwasher (don't use a standard home dishwasher);
- storage shelving;
- cool work surface for cold food and salad prep away from ovens;
- work surfaces for prepping food and surfaces for food processors, for example;
- hanging pot and pan rack to increase storage space preferably by stoves;
- good, accessible storage for cooking equipment;
- good lighting and decent air flow;
- telephone if the kitchen is far away from the office space.

It is also worth considering a microwave, a steamer, a griddle, a convection oven for pastry, a professional ice cream maker and other refrigeration and freezers.

Cookers

Gas or electricity? As any cook worth his or her salt will tell you, gas is far preferable as it can be regulated so much more finely than electricity. A combination of gas burners and an electric oven is one many chefs like.

In convection ovens, fans distribute the heat evenly, taking away the necessity of moving items around for uniform cooking. Baking temperatures are usually lower.

Buying kitchen equipment

Look for good, solid equipment on castors for easy cleaning, and consider second-hand equipment for cutting down the cost of the kitchen. But buy sensibly, not just because it's a bargain. It may not be a few months down the line.

If you are taking over a catering premises there may be suitable equipment included in the price. If so, make sure all is in working order, establish who services the equipment, get any attached paperwork from the seller of the business and insist that it is cleaned thoroughly before you take over the property.

If buying from specialists, ask for training to be given to kitchen staff who should be familiar with most, if not all, of the equipment.

◆ TIP ◆

Always have a commercial dishwasher installed. It takes a fraction of the time of a domestic one, and the interior is designed without frills to fit in the maximum dishes or pots and pans. There is usually a separate tray for glass washing.

Leasing equipment

Small businesses simply can't afford to buy equipment unless they have acquired good financial backing and, as a result, leasing equipment is a good, viable option. All kinds of equipment can be leased – from vans to computers and refrigeration to office furniture – to help the business get up and running.

A lease is normally a long-term involvement to rent equipment, although it can be negotiated with the leasing company if they are flexible. They are, in turn, responsible for the maintenance of the equipment and will replace faulty items. All items are returned to the company at the end of the lease or sometimes you can to purchase them outright.

Although leasing is a help to get started, it can be more of an expense in the long term so do your homework and look into the costs of buying out-right or leasing. If leasing, as you don't own the piece of equipment in the long run, you can't sell it. And, buyer beware: a lease is a long-term obliga-tion, the cancellation fees as much as if you had used the equipment for the whole leasing period. If you try to get out of a lease, the penalties can be far-reaching, even to the extent of giving you a negative credit rating which could throw your business into difficulties.

COOKING EQUIPMENT

You may not need all the items on this list if, for example, you make sandwiches, cakes or condiments. You can always buy equipment as you need it rather than stocking up on items which will increase your start-up costs.

General:

- ◆ apple corer
- ◆ cast iron casseroles with lids
- ◆ cheese grater
- ◆ chinois (fine sieve)
- ◆ chopping boards (see EHO guidelines)
- ◆ corkscrew
- ◆ fish pan
- ◆ fish slice
- ◆ funnel
- ◆ graters
- ◆ heavy based saucepans for sauces etc
- ◆ heavy based stock pots
- ◆ heavy duty cast iron frying pans
- ◆ kitchen scales
- ◆ kitchen scissors
- ◆ knives for many uses (see page 41)
- ◆ ladles
- ◆ large spoons
- ◆ lemon squeezer
- ◆ lemon zester
- ◆ mandoline
- ◆ measuring jugs
- ◆ mixing bowls of all sizes
- ◆ nutmeg grater
- ◆ pancake pan
- ◆ pastry brushes
- ◆ pepper and salt mill
- ◆ plastic lidded containers for food storage and labels

- roasting and baking trays
- saute pans, shallow pans, dutch ovens (for braising, sautéing or stews)
- sieves and colanders
- slotted spoons
- spatulas
- steamer
- terrines, ramekin dishes
- tin opener
- tongs
- vegetable peelers
- whisks
- and anything else that is suited to the food you produce!

Nozzles and brushes:

- piping nozzles, plain and fluted
- selection of plastic piping for cutting into ring moulds
- 36cm/14 inch plastic piping bag and nozzles
- poly spray bottles for oil
- ruler
- selection of brushes.

Tins and trays:

- cake tins of various sizes with (essential!) removable bases
- baking tray, non-stick, of various sizes
- muffin tins
- cooling racks
- dariole moulds
- roasting tins.

Electrical goods:

- blender (a heavy duty one and simple to clean)
- coffee grinders (one for spices, one for coffee beans)

- deep-fat fryer
- hand whisk with a variety of whisks
- juicer.

Other basic equipment:

- tea towels – lots!
- hand towels
- catering packs of foil, cling film and silicon paper
- bags – rubbish and freezer
- cleaning materials
- dishcloths
- antibacterial spray
- heavy-duty bins.

Knives:

- large chopping knife
- sharpening steel or electric/water sharpener
- palette knife
- carving knife
- chef's knife – 15 cm
- medium knife – 20–25 cm
- filleting knife (for fish)
- several paring knives (like a vegetable knife)
- potato peeler
- meat cleaver
- ham slicer with supple blade
- boning knife
- salmon knife
- bread knife
- cooking fork.

Knife tips

It never pays to buy cheap knives. Some excellent brands are Gustav, Emil & Ern, Sabatier, Sheffield Steel, Victorinox, Ed. Wustof and my favourite, J.A. Henkels. I still have cherished knives from my 1980s restaurant days which, despite the outlay, are in excellent condition and are as effective as the day they were bought. If you are hiring a chef or chefs, they will often provide their own sets which have been built up over their career.

◆ High carbon, stainless steel knives won't discolour or rust but will need more sharpening. The sharpest knives are made from carbon steel but can discolour when slicing onions or other acidic food.
◆ If a carbon steel knife is badly discoloured, wet it, sprinkle with kitchen salt and rub vigorously with a cut lemon. A piece of burnt cork is useful for rusty knives.
◆ Keep knives on a wall-mounted rack, never in a drawer with other equipment
◆ Wash and dry knives immediately. Never soak them.
◆ Keep knives sharp at all times. Inexperienced staff using blunt knives can injure themselves.
◆ Look in the *Yellow Pages* for knife sharpeners who do the restaurant kitchen rounds or invest in an electric/water sharpener for in-house sharpening.

HIRING EQUIPMENT

Most caterers don't invest in plates, cups, saucers, knives, forks, spoons, glasses and other equipment for setting up tables as it is a) expensive to do and to replace, especially if the pattern is no longer made, and b) a hassle to transport around and to clean at outside catering jobs.

Instead, many caterers use hire companies and pass on the expense of the hire to the customers. This way, it isn't necessary to find precious storage space or to worry about broken glasses, chipped plates and missing teaspoons.

What hire companies offer

Visit a number of companies to see what they offer, and get their brochures. When you find a good, reliable company, it is worth its weight in gold. They deliver when you stipulate (by arrangement with the customer) and collect everything dirty the following day (or when arranged for). This is especially valuable if you are catering for a party in a marquee with no running water and with no possibility of washing even a tea cup.

If you want to cut costs, there are cheaper hire companies where you are responsible for collection and delivery of the equipment, plus returning it all in spotless condition.

Be aware that hire companies will charge for breakages and loss. They can be hefty charges so make sure that when, for example, your staff are clearing plates with cutlery on them, they don't throw anything out with an uneaten potato or slice of cake.

As well as several patterns of plates, glassware and cutlery, hire companies offer some of the following:

- table linen
- napkins
- cafetieres
- specialist glassware and canapé coloured glassware
- non-slip drinks trays
- water boilers
- large pans, roasting tins
- plate stackers (tiered for a large number of guests so that courses can be plated and on hold in a small area prior to serving)
- tables and trestle tables
- chairs
- industrial cookers, fridges, barbecues
- dustbins (useful for keeping drinks chilled, as well as the obvious).

You can, of course, hire glasses from supermarkets and wine merchants, the 'free' hire dependant on the purchase of wine and other alcohol. Some offer the dull, disappointing Paris goblets (the wine is unable to breathe properly in these little glasses). Vote with your feet and buy your wine from a better retailer who not only has preferable wine but also much better glassware. Majestic Wine, for example, has proper wine glasses with a thinner rim, and champagne glasses.

If you obtain glasses this way you have to collect them and give them a good polish with a clean tea towel before using, or a wash. A final wash, rinse and dry before returning them to the shop is part of the deal.

Cost

Before agreeing to hire, you need to ensure that the amount of equipment needed is sourced and quoted for and the customer is made aware of the full cost (make sure the VAT is added too). Some caterers add a handling charge for this service but I see it as a necessary service to the customer and don't, the invoice going directly to the customer from the hire company.

Deciding what you need

Make sure you go through the menu with a fine toothcomb to ensure that you have enough serving dishes, serving spoons and glasses (are the guests being offered several types of wine plus water and other drinks, for example?) and other equipment, so you don't have the embarrassment of not being able to set up the tables or a buffet properly.

Talking to the client

If your hire company has a brochure with pictures of each item, show it to clients to ensure their approval. If your client is on a tight budget, offer them a choice of equipment hire as a) they may wish to spend as little as possible or b) it may not be the smartest of occasions.

STORAGE AND REFRIGERATION

Many caterers who don't have regular contracts (in contrast to those who know what they are doing the entire working week), only buy food in when they have successfully negotiated a job, be it a wedding, corporate event or a dinner party. Of course you have the basics, such as sugar, flour, dried pasta, rice, salt, pepper and other ingredients that aren't perishable. If working from home, these are stored for catering purposes in a separate area from food for home use. Everything must be kept off the floor in sealable containers to protect the food from pests.

Refrigeration

You must have refrigeration specifically for your catering. Home food and food destined for clients mustn't be stored together. Make sure that the refrigeration is up to the job, that it can maintain the required temperature at 4°C and that it isn't rusty or in poor condition. The interior must be spotless and remain that way.

When putting food that you have prepared in the fridge, label everything and include whose party it is for, the date and who made it (if there are several of you cooking).

Freezers

I really recommend that you have two, smaller, freezers rather than one large one. When you aren't busy, you can turn the unused one off, and save on running costs. If – heaven forbid! – one freezer packs up, you can store your produce in the other one.

Make sure that your freezer or freezers are in the same good condition as the refrigeration. I deliberately have very little freezing space as I believe that everything I offer to clients must be made for them and them alone; a freezer is just for home-made ice cream and freezer packs to take along to keep some foods chilled.

But if your business relies on frozen ingredients, do make absolutely sure that you keep a list of what food you have – and on which shelves it is stored – so that you can save yourself frustration and time trying to locate an item, only to find that you used it for a previous function. A written inventory is a life saver.

Make sure too that everything that goes into your freezer is labelled and sufficiently wrapped for life in the freezer. Label and date everything that is placed in your freezer. Have a regular inventory, and throw out items frozen beyond their sell-by date rather than keeping them to pass on to unsuspecting customers. This is very bad practice and is deeply frowned upon by not only environmental health officers but caterers too. Take a deep breath and chuck it out, or use it for your own use if you think it is safe.

Perishable goods

Store your vegetables and fruit that don't need refrigeration (onions, potatoes, lemons, melons for example) in a dedicated dry area away from light and heat so that they don't deteriorate quickly. You want all your ingredients as fresh as possible so that when you start cooking, you're not tossing food out before you've used it. Think about where you will store your perishable goods. If you're taking over the garden shed, is it clean enough, does it get the full force of the sun or is it in a cool, shady spot? Is there adequate ventilation? These principles apply to wherever you store the goods.

Wastage

The key to a good catering operation is to know how much food to buy so that wastage doesn't occur. Easier said than done, I know, especially when you are starting in the business and have no catering experience, but you will soon be an expert at ordering and storing as it means the difference between making a profit and losing valuable assets.

Containers

When buying plastic containers for storage, make sure that you get boxes that will last, that are well made and easily cleanable. Check that the lids are easy to remove. Hunt around for quality plastic and don't go to high street stores to buy your containers without looking at wholesale and cash and carry outlets beforehand. Or go directly to the manufacturers if you are buying a large number of containers. You can never have enough!

> ◆ TIP ◆
>
> Keep your storage in pristine order so that you can put freshly-made food into the containers at a moment's notice.

TRANSPORTING THE FOOD

If funds are available and you think catering is for you, do buy a suitable vehicle. If not, you car will do as a means of transportation for smaller events but it will need to be spotless. If it is used for carrying pets around it won't be suitable unless you scrub it down every time within an inch of its life before you use it for food transportation. The interior of your vehicle should be as clean as your kitchen.

Making a good impression

Eventually, you will need to buy a professional-looking and practical vehicle if you wish to project the right image for your business. Early in my catering career I recall arriving in a small car at one function, a 50th wedding anniversary, the daughters of the happy pair sniffily telling me that I didn't look like a caterer as I unloaded the car despite its cleanliness. Did I take this as a compliment or not?

Obviously, the first impressions of your business matters, and a sad, old vehicle doesn't conjure up a picture of glorious food hygienically handled for the function. That old adage of not being able to judge a book by its cover just can't and shouldn't apply here.

Packing the vehicle

You will learn to become an expert packer of your vehicle, but still buy a vehicle that is just a little larger than you think you will need. If you are catering for a larger party than you normally do, there are two options: hire a van to suit the event or ask staff to transport some of the equipment. But do make sure that if the food is going into any of their vehicles, the interiors are as clean as necessary to transport food.

I never carry food ready to be served but always move the food onto serving dishes or plates from containers at the venue. It is asking for trouble to carry platters of ready-to-serve food as damage to the food is a distinct possibility during transit.

4

Health and Safety

As a caterer, you need to know about the Food Safety Act and Regulations as well as what types of food poisoning exist and how to avoid them. This chapter covers these topics, safety tips, how to transport food and also the role of the environmental health officer.

It is a legal requirement that anyone involved in food preparation in the UK holds a basic food hygiene preparation certificate. Contact your local environmental health officer for details and types of courses.

◆ TIP ◆

In Scotland the regulations apply slightly differently to the rest of the UK but the principles are the same. Contact your local authority for more information.

The Food Safety Act 1990

Under this act you must not:

◆ sell (or keep for sale) food that is unfit for people to eat;
◆ cause food to be dangerous to health;
◆ sell food that is not what the customer is entitled to expect, in terms of content or quality;
◆ describe or present food in a way that is false or misleading.

Food Safety (General Food Hygiene) Regulations 1995

This act covers food hygiene training:

◆ anyone who handles open food in the course of a food business must receive food hygiene training;
◆ short courses levels are foundation, intermediate and advanced. You can find out what courses are available from your local authority.

Food Safety (Temperature Control) Regulations 1995

This refers to:

◆ the temperature at which certain foods must be kept;
◆ which foods are exempt from specific temperature control.

FRIDGE STORAGE AND TEMPERATURE CONTROL

◆ TIP ◆

Foods that need temperature control must be kept either HOT at or above 63°C or COLD at or below 8°C.

Temperature control is essential in food storage. It is vital that raw meat is, for example, stored at the base of the fridge at a temperature of 1–4°C to stop bacteria from multiplying. Keep a thermometer in the fridge and record a diary of temperatures for health and safety inspection. Keep it on the door to remind staff to check the temperature levels.

Other foods that need chilling are:

◆ Milk, yoghurt, cream, butter, foods with cream filling, dairy-based deserts and certain cheeses.
◆ Many cooked products until ready to eat cold or heated. Most foods containing eggs, meat, fish, dairy products, cereals, rice, pulses or vegetables, and sandwich fillings containing these ingredients.
◆ Most smoked or cured products like hams unless the curing method means the product is not perishable at room temperature.
◆ Prepared ready-to-eat meals including prepared vegetables, salad leaves, coleslaw and products containing mayonnaise.
◆ Pizzas with meat, fish or vegetables.
◆ Foods with 'use by' and 'keep refrigerated' labels.

Foods that don't need chilling:

◆ Some cured/smoked products.
◆ Bakery goods.
◆ Canned and dried foods like pickles, jams, sauces. (However, these do need chilling once opened.)

◆ TIP ◆

Mail order food must not be transported at temperatures that could cause a health risk; food that needs chilling should be delivered by chilled compartment vehicle.

FOOD POISONING

As a caterer you and your staff need to understand what causes food poisoning and how it can be avoided. It is vital that your premises are clean throughout. The kitchen, naturally, is the hot spot where cleanliness is of paramount importance. The food you serve must be absolutely safe; you can do this by strict following of hygiene and cross contamination rules.

Below are the most common causes of food poisoning. It makes for alarming reading! But remember that they are preventable.

◆ **Campylobactor:** the most common food poisoning bug in the UK. Found in raw and undercooked poultry, red meat, unpasteurised milk, untreated water. Just a piece of undercooked chicken can cause severe illness.
Symptoms: gastroenteritis with fever, abdominal cramps and diarrhoea that is often bloody. Can be fatal.

◆ **Salmonella:** the second most common food poisoning bug. Found in eggs, raw meat, poultry, unpasteurised milk, yeast and even pasta, coconut and chocolate. Grows very well in the food itself unless the food is chilled. It is also passed easily from person to person by poor hygiene such as not washing hands.
Symptoms: usually mild, with abdominal pain, diarrhoea and nausea but rarely vomiting.

◆ **Clostridium perfringens:** the third most common bug and the least reported as symptoms are vague. Found in soil, sewage, animal manure and in the gut of animals and humans. It breeds in food cooked slowly in large quantities then left to stand for a long time.
Symptoms: when taken in large numbers, the bacteria produce toxins which attack the gut lining causing diarrhoea and acute abdominal pain.

◆ **Listeria:** a food poisoning bug of particular danger to pregnant women, babies and the elderly. Found in soft, mould-ripened cheeses, pates, unpasteurised milk and shellfish. Resists heat, salt and nitrate and acidity better than many micro-organisms.
Symptoms: fever, headache, nausea and vomiting. Can be fatal to the elderly, immune impaired infants and developing foetuses.

◆ **Scrombotoxin:** although not strictly speaking a bug, this poison is produced by certain bacteria in oily fish which has been allowed to spoil through inadequate refrigeration. It causes a dramatic histamine reaction. Found in fresh and tinned mackerel, tuna and – very rarely – Swiss cheese.

Symptoms: tingling or burning in the mouth, a rash on the face or upper body, itching, sweating and headache with a drop in blood pressure, abdominal pain, diarrhoea and vomiting.

◆ **E.coli 0157:** most strains of E.coli are harmless but those producing the poison verocytoxin can cause severe illness, E.coli 0157 being one. Found in farm animals and land contaminated with their faeces. Transmitted through undercooked minced beef (such as burgers) and unpasturised, inadequately heated or contaminated milk.
Symptoms: abdominal cramps and bloody diarrhoea. In serious cases, kidney failure, severe anaemia, neurological problems and death.

Avoiding contamination

In order to combat food poisoning, obtain good clear advice from your local authority health inspector. All of the above are perfectly preventable if you are aware of them and how they can be avoided. Poisonings by salmonella and campylobacter are, however, on the increase due to a lack of understanding by those handling food.

Lack of common sense, too, features. Leaving raw chicken out in a hot kitchen for four hours without covering it is asking for trouble. It should be covered and refrigerated, of course. Don't, for example, prepare a sandwich on a board which has just been used for cutting up raw duck breasts or other poultry or raw meat.

◆ **EXPERIENCE** ◆

Remember the case of the caterer at wedding who left the entire buffet laid out in a hot marquee for over four hours while the many and varied pictures of the happy couple and their family were taken. It resulted in mass, serious, food-poisoning.

It's a good idea to use heavy-duty plastic or polypropylene colour-coded boards. Thoroughly scrub in hot, soapy water and rinse after use to avoid cross-contamination and food poisoning. Or use an antibacterial spray with a paper kitchen towel.

> **◆ TIP ◆**
>
> Ask your local environmental health officer about the use of wooden boards. They are now returning to kitchens as plastic boards can be damaged by knives as easily as wooden ones. Plastic ones are also very hard on knives, causing them to require more sharpening.

Eggs have been under scrutiny for many years. Health and safety guidelines suggest that raw or semi-cooked eggs may pose a salmonella food poisoning problem. All recipes printed in newspapers, magazines and books carry a warning not to serve undercooked eggs to the elderly or women who are pregnant.

You may decide that is not worth the worry – out of the window may go some of the most wonderful egg dishes such as Eggs Benedict, poached or lightly scrambled eggs and Hollandaise sauce. It is up to you to make this decision to serve eggs that aren't thoroughly cooked. If your client requests egg dishes, be sure that they understand the issues.

> **◆ TIP ◆**
>
> If space is an issue in your refrigeration, you may have to re-think what you can offer as a caterer if some items are not able to be refrigerated for any length of time.

HYGIENE STANDARDS

Hygiene in all parts of your catering operation must be of the highest order. You need to think about it when working in your kitchen and storage area, and other environments such as someone else's home, a marquee, at a farmers' market or any other outside catering premises.

When working in someone's home, for example, and preparing a dinner, buffet or canapés, I arrange beforehand with the client that surfaces should be cleared. Then always clean the surfaces, sink and surrounding area before you start any kind of work. Even if it looks pristine, a spray of disinfectant and a clean cloth gives you peace of mind. I always work on the premise that maybe a cat has roamed on the kitchen tops and while this seems normal to the household, to a caterer it's a no-no.

Top tips for food hygiene

◆ Cover food left to cool to avoid contamination and attracting flies.

◆ Make sure all containers are cleaned properly before storage and re-checked before use.

◆ Don't take chances with food that has been unrefrigerated for a long time after a function. Throw it out, especially if in a warm environment.

◆ Don't put food still warm from cooking in the fridge but wait until cooled otherwise the fridge's temperature will rise and bacteria will grow.

◆ Cover food in the fridge with a lid, foil or cling film to avoid drying out and cross-contamination. Always store cooked and raw meat and fish on separate shelves.

◆ Don't wrap cheese or meats in cling film but in greaseproof paper. That way they won't sweat and will keep fresh longer.

◆ When storing salad leaves and herbs, add a layer of kitchen paper to the lidded container to soak up any excess moisture.

◆ Always tidy up your kitchen space, wash your surfaces thoroughly and do the washing up before starting on another dish. This way, you will minimise any risk of cross contamination and help the smooth running of your kitchen.

◆ After each function, mini spring-clean your fridge and throw out any unlabelled items that you are not sure of or any foodstuffs that have lost their allure. Be thrifty: make soup with those leftover vegetables.

◆ Make a point of labelling anything that goes into your fridge with contents, date and use by instructions. Never take chances with your livelihood or your clients' health.

◆ Check those dried herbs and spices. Sell-by date well and truly passed? Toss and replace. Buy in small quantities and store in a cool, dark, dry place.

◆ Keep your records and cookbooks out of the kitchen if at all possible. They pick up moisture and grease and can become damaged and unusable.

Staff hygiene

It is vital that any staff you employ, permanent or temporary (waiting staff at a function, for example), are aware of hygiene.

Staff must always wash their hands after using the toilet, using soap and clean towels. It's a good idea to have a reminder notice in the toilets. Hand washing also must take place to avoid cross contamination after handling raw poultry, for example. If kitchen staff nip out to check on storage or to have a cigarette or coffee break they must wash their hands before resuming work.

Staff must be aware of other personal hygiene matters too, such as not touching the face, nose, ears, hair or other parts of the body while working as it can spread infection and micro-organisms. It's a good idea for staff to wear a hat, as well as catering gloves, while preparing or plating up food.

Staff employed to work at functions must wash their hands before starting work and follow the personal hygiene rules above.

◆ TIP ◆

Staff should wash their hands in basins that are used just for this purpose, not where food is washed or equipment cleaned.

Cloths

Dishcloths and other cloths in the kitchen are one of the prime ways to spread germs. Use non-woven dishcloths rather than sponges as there are fewer traps for germs. Sponges also hold more water where bacteria can thrive.

Don't even think of using a cloth which is used on a counter to mop up the floor, then use it again for surface tops. Disinfect cloths in bleach regularly and dry flat, not scrunched up. Be a devil and throw them away after quite extensive use!

◆ TIP ◆

Change tea towels and hand towels often.

ENVIRONMENTAL HEALTH REQUIREMENTS

The role of the environmental health officer

Catering kitchens take a physical hammering, and there is a huge amount of effort needed to promote the best standards of hygiene, cleanliness, stock care and food rotation. Take your eye off the ball – and your staff –

and you could land up with a big problem, with food poisoning the out-come. Witness Gordon Ramsay's television programme Kitchen Nightmares to see how poorly-run some restaurant kitchens can be. This also applies to catering premises.

The policing of standards is down to environmental health officers from local councils who enforce the law. Although some in the trade think the laws are draconian and requirements over the top, the system can't be bucked. Some of the requests are legally binding, others aren't. But their advice can be invaluable, particularly for those starting up in the business or those whose standards have slipped.

> **◆ TIP ◆**
>
> Environmental health officers can, by law, turn up unannounced at all reasonable hours to inspect your catering premises including toilets, storage space and your rubbish area. They may also visit due to a complaint.

Some of the many items they will inspect are lids and labels on containers, the use of the right chopping boards, and fridge and freezer temperatures. They will take a keen interest in the suitability and cleanliness of tiles, floor, walls and ceilings, storage, hand basins for staff, how raw and cooked meat are stored in the fridge, air circulation and vermin problems.

There are EHO horror stories: finding stoves with no knobs on, staff turning the gas on with pliers, dirty stale oil left in fryers and filthy fridges with no labelling on containers. They have also discovered babies' soiled nappies left in the kitchen, mould and mice droppings behind equipment, fire doors propped open with unsealed rubbish and cleaning fluids transferred to lemonade bottles.

What to do when your business is inspected

Some premises are inspected every six months, the majority much less often. An inspector will show identification before carrying out an inspection, and then give feedback, for example, about identified hazards and guidance on how they can be avoided.

If there is problem, you will be given the reasons in writing for any action you are asked to take. Where there is an apparent breach of law, it will be explained and you are given reasonable time to meet statutory require-ments, except when there is an immediate risk to public health. You will also be informed of the procedures for appealing against local authority action as a matter of course.

You have nothing to be concerned about if you use your common sense when running your business.

Inspectors' powers

They can take samples and photographs, and inspect records. They will write informally to ask you to put right any problems they find. They may serve you with an improvement order where breaches of the law are iden-tified which must be put right. They can detain or seize goods and, in serious cases, they may recommend a prosecution. If there is an imminent health risk to consumers, inspectors can serve an emergency prohibition order which forbids the use of the premises or equipment which is backed up by the law court.

Measures that can be taken if you disagree with the outcome

In the unlikely event of being prosecuted, here are guidelines to take. (I can't stress enough that if you follow sensible precautions, your business will not come under such stringent scrutiny.)

- ◆ Contact your local authority's head of environmental health or trading standards services to see if the matter can be resolved informally. If dis-agreement remains, contact your local councillor.
- ◆ Contact your local authority or trade association if you think the law is being applied differently to other authorities. Ask about LACOTS (Local Authorities Co-ordinating Body on Food and Trading Standards.)
- ◆ You have the right of appeal to a magistrates' court against an improve-ment notice or a refusal by a local authority to lift an emergency prohibition order made earlier by the court.
- ◆ A magistrates' court must confirm the emergency closure of a business or the seizure of food. If magistrates decide premises have been shut

down without proper reason or food has been wrongly seized or detained, you have a right to compensation.

Other things that are taken into consideration are:

◆ the seriousness of the offence;
◆ the inspectors' confidence in the restaurant's management;
◆ the consequences of non compliance;
◆ the attitude of the operator/proprietor.

◆ TIP ◆

Your local authority is ready to help if you need any advice on food safety. Trade associations and independent consultancy services can also help.

SAFETY IN THE KITCHEN

The following lists are basically common sense but, as a chef in charge of the kitchen or a proprietor, you are obliged to pass these basic safety precautions on to all staff taking part in food preparation and the servicing of food.

Hot food and liquids
◆ Don't leave metal implements such as spoons in boiling liquids.
◆ Don't overfill coffee pots, soup tureens etc, with hot liquids.
◆ Get help when carrying large or heavy containers of hot food.
◆ Don't use a damp cloth to carry hot utensils.

Cookers and electrical equipment
◆ Don't leave handles of cooking pans over gas flames or leave them over the front of cookers or on surfaces.
◆ Always remove the plug prior to cleaning electrical equipment.
◆ Turn off all gas and electrical appliances when not in use.
◆ Dangerous machinery such as meat slices need to be adequately guarded.
◆ Avoid reaching over naked flames or hot plates.
◆ Never pour water on a fat or oil fire but smother it with a fire blanket or a thick damp sack.

Knives

◆ When carrying knives hold the point downwards.

◆ Never attempt to catch a falling knife.

◆ Always use sharp knives. Blunt knives cause accidents because you have to apply too much pressure.

◆ Cut or chop on a board, never in the hand.

Spillages and other accidents

◆ Clean up any spillages immediately.

◆ Broken glass needs to be wrapped up well before going into the bin.

◆ Avoid putting debris from ashtrays into bins containing paper as some of the cigarette ash may still be alight.

◆ Have a first aid box handy and topped up with sufficient waterproof dressings and burns dressings. Be sure everyone knows where it is stored.

Other equipment and storage

◆ Avoid the use of trays for multi-stacking of clean equipment. Instead, use one tray for cutlery, one for glasses etc.

◆ Never put cleaning or any other fluids in bottles originally used for food or drink or use cups, glasses, soup bowls etc for storing cleaning agents.

◆ TIP ◆

Have a check list of procedures to carry out when food preparation has ended, for example, gas off, fridge door shut properly, back door locked, rubbish bags removed or tied to avoid pests.

TRANSPORTING FOOD

When you transport food from one premises to another – from cash and carry back to your premises, from your business to a catering venue for example – it is vital to keep it from becoming contaminated with dirt or bacteria.

Make sure that:

◆ food is transported in suitable packaging or containers to prevent contamination (not in used plastic bags or open containers, for example);
◆ chilled foods are kept at the right temperature either by using cool bags or boxes or by refrigerated vans;
◆ containers are not used for transporting anything other than foodstuffs as it may result in contamination;
◆ raw and cooked foods are kept separate at all times;
◆ vehicles used to transport food are kept clean and in good repair;
◆ food is labelled – when you get to your destination you will know what needs to be refrigerated and what needs to be kept cool, for example.

FURTHER INFORMATION AND USEFUL CONTACTS

You can get more information from the Food Standards Agency, a UK-wide independent government agency providing advice and information to the public and government on food safety, diet and nutrition (www.food.gov.uk).

They publish the following leaflets:

◆ 'Food Safety Regulations': a general guide to regulations on food hygiene and temperature control.
◆ 'Food Law Inspections and Your Business': explains the inspection process.
◆ 'Food Handlers: Fitness to Work': explains what to do when staff have certain types of illness.
◆ 'Eggs: What Caterers Need to Know': gives advice for caterers on using eggs safely.
◆ 'Dine Out, Eat Well': a guide to offering customers healthy choices.

All of these publications are free of charge. To order copies, contact Food Standards Agency Publications on 0845 606 0667 or email: foodstandards@eclogistics.co.uk.

Other publications available from the government:

◆ 'Small Business Service'
◆ 'Small Firms: Setting up in Business'
◆ 'Small Firms: Employing Staff'
◆ 'Small Firms: Health and Safety'.

To order, call 0870 150 2500 or email: publications@dti.gso.gov.uk. Or you can visit www.dti.gov.uk/publications.

Also of help from the Health and Safety Executive:

◆ 'Health and Safety Executive: Working with Employers'
◆ 'Managing Heath and Safety pay in the Catering Industry'
◆ 'Planning for Health and Safety when selecting and using Catering Equipment and Workplaces'
◆ 'The Main Health and Safety Law Applicable to Catering'.

Order from www.hsebooks.co.uk, call 01787 882265 or access publications online at www.hse.gov.uk.

5

Business Finances

When you are thinking about starting your catering business, it's easy to be put off by the daunting task of organising your finances. But, as any business person knows, this crucial part of your business must be dealt with meticulously, and on a regular, on-going basis.

If you don't have a head for figures, make sure that you have a partner who does or that you can rely on an accountant to deal with the necessary sums.

This chapter covers:

◆ your business plan;
◆ talking to banks;
◆ finding other sources of financing;

- overheads and costs;
- bookkeeping, accountancy and financial records;
- methods of payment for suppliers and from customers;
- insurance;
- business rates;
- VAT;
- staff wages, the national minimum wage and pensions.

I'll try to make this as engaging and informative as possible. Pay attention at the back!

YOUR BUSINESS PLAN

Having a business plan is not only important for your bank, it's also a great way to focus your ideas and work out if what you're planning really is viable.

The first thing you need to do is work out an initial proposal. In this you will need to include:

- name and location;
- who your customers will be;
- content of the menu and drinks list;
- staffing costs;
- purchase costs;
- rental;
- projected income.

Business plans are, of course, not a guarantee for success but they help to identify the strengths and weaknesses of an idea, and will greatly improve your chances of succeeding. When you have finished your initial proposal, you can build on it to create a more detailed plan. You should include the following information.

Introduction: your catering business' purpose, your expertise and history and those of your partners, your staff (should you have a chef lined up, for example, if you're not doing the cooking yourself?), your Unique Selling Point (what is going to make it work and make it different?)

Executive summary: this describes the business in general terms. Make this short and to the point to make it easy for others to follow.

Overview: your mission. What are you looking to achieve? Why do you think it will work? Make this as clear and as short as possible too.

Business environment: market research into your type of catering business, its potential location, problems and possible solutions, the competition and expansion potential (selling at farmers' markets, for example).

If you are asking for a bank loan make your presentation professional-looking. A messy jumble of ideas randomly put on paper will not improve anyone's chances of getting to the next stage of discussions. Instead, choose a business-like font, put ideas under headings, check the spelling and present it in a titled folder with perhaps some clear drawings. Make several copies to hand out.

ESTIMATING YOUR START-UP COSTS

First of all, estimate your start-up costs. These checklists are a guideline.

Your capital costs:

- your business premises (if not run from home);
- the equipment needed to start your business (see Chapter 3);
- your marketing tools (e.g. printing of cards and menus, telephone, mobile, website, computer, printer);
- initial office supplies (e.g. filing cabinet, bookkeeping book);
- basic food and supplies (start-up basic ingredients such as dry goods – salt, pepper, flour, rice, pasta);
- required tools (see Chapter 3);
- any legal costs if setting up dedicated premises;
- accountancy costs;
- loan charges if applicable.

Once you have made a list of these items, make a list of the estimated operating costs:

♦ utility costs (water, electricity, gas);
♦ insurance coverage;
♦ business rates (if applicable);
♦ employee salaries;
♦ rent (if applicable);
♦ taxes;
♦ equipment maintenance (put a sum aside for this).

How much do I need?

Once your catering operation is up and running with initial start-up costs covered, you will be in business. You will have an income and, with this, expenses. You will need to establish whether you have sufficient capital to deal with expenses for at least the first three months of business. A six-month reserve is, of course, even more desirable.

A significant number of small businesses fail because they are under-capitalised, i.e. they start off without enough backing to pay monthly fixed expenses when the business isn't up to its fighting weight. Make sure you do your budgeting carefully and thoroughly before venturing into business.

The following things will help as well:

♦ Having a working husband/wife/partner who can cover household expenses while your business gets going; or if you are able to support yourself during the start-up months.
♦ Having some clients already in the pipeline to start your business. If you do, when can you expect payment? If it's a month or two down the line, cash flow will become a problem. Think about what else you can do.
♦ Keeping your operating costs at a bare minimum until you are established.

ESTIMATING YOUR BUSINESS FINANCE

It is important to estimate as accurately as you can but sometimes you just have to guess in business, however unsound that seems. Forecasting exactly how many catering jobs you will get is difficult.

When you are estimating, think about the following.

♦ **Are your projections believable** and based on facts? Get someone (a friend who is in a profitable business, for example) who is knowledgeable about figures to check your projected costs as you may have missed something out. They might see a flaw or agree that you're on the right track.

♦ **Beware of carrying too much stock.** There is no need to have too much of anything as you will buy in stocks for a specific event. You may be tempted to buy in some bargain wine, for example. But you must bear in mind that you may not be able to sell it on if it isn't what the customer wants.

♦ **Don't underestimate.** Underestimating a catering package for a specific event can mean less profit or, worse case scenario, a loss. With experience you will become a master of estimating everything from how many rolls you will need to bags of ice.

♦ **Always estimate each and every cost** including rent, rates, staff, travel costs and insurance for example.

♦ **Don't forget quarterly expenses** – e.g. telephone, utilities, bank charges.

♦ **Payment.** Will it be immediately after the event or a month or two down the line? Put your stipulated trading conditions on the quote and ask for a deposit. For example, if it is a big function, ask for 50 per cent up front, the remainder to be paid within 28 days. For a small function such as a dinner party for ten, I always present the bill at the end of the evening (having discussed with the customer in the confirmation letter when payment is due).

♦ Always review your finances and re-consider your options. Can you find a better rate for a loan? Avoid financing that is too complex.

YOUR ASSETS AND LIABILITIES

But before you go to the bank with your business plan for your catering business, you need to think about your net financial worth. What are your assets and liabilities?

Assets: What do you have, either short or long term? A short-term asset is what you have in your bank account, or something that can be turned into cash within a short period of time. If it can't be available for the foreseeable future, i.e. for several years, then it's a long-term asset. Examples of assets are stocks, bonds, saving certificates and premium bonds. Also your car, house, furniture, jewellery and equipment.

Liabilities: A liability is something you are responsible for financially. For example:

◆ any outstanding loans;
◆ credit card payments;
◆ instalments on furniture, appliances and other household items;
◆ outstanding taxes;
◆ mortgage.

Your assets should be greater than your liabilities. Go to your bank for advice on how you can calculate this, and then you will be clearer as to how to proceed in financing your venture. You may discover you don't have enough to start your business, or you might have enough to put into reserve until the business really gets going.

DEALING WITH SEASONAL PEAKS AND TROUGHS

If you have only been involved in a large catering business, it may come as an unwelcome surprise that for small to medium catering businesses the work is very seasonal.

Generally speaking, catering companies make their profits during the obvious times of the year: Christmas, Easter, summer and summer weddings. The rest of the year is punctuated by other smaller catering jobs in the corporate or private sector. Naturally, this fluctuation is difficult to handle, and post-Christmas blues often set in.

This is your time to:

◆ take a break;
◆ do some effective marketing;

- ◆ train staff;
- ◆ paint the kitchen;
- ◆ try out new suppliers;
- ◆ create new menus;
- ◆ keep in contact with customers by sending out these new menus;
- ◆ set up some cookery classes;
- ◆ get to grips with your accounting.

It is, therefore, essential to put some of the profits you have made during busy periods by so that essential bills can be paid and that there is adequate cash flow. Put some of those profits into a saving account so that it isn't unintentionally frittered away.

CALCULATING MENU COSTINGS

It is essential to cost your menus to build in a profit margin. In order to do this, you need to know the cost of each item that goes into a dish. This includes the butter or oil you may have used for the preparation of the dish, the garnish and the seasoning. Take into account tax and VAT (if you are not VAT exempt).

> **◆ TIP ◆**
>
> Your gross profit – GP as it is known in the trade – is vital to get right.

The average GP (total profit) is 60 per cent, your costs being 40 per cent. (If you are running a more upmarket catering company and sourcing top quality produce, aim at 65 per cent GP.)

Some items will be cheaper and quicker than others to prepare. For example, a bacon and mushroom salad is cheaper and quicker to make than a salmon and prawn terrine. Lower the GP on expensive dishes and increase the GP on the cheaper dishes to make more profit. This is loss-leader practice, and is done by catering companies, supermarkets and other retail businesses.

The net profit (the profit after all costs have been taken out) is then calculated. The cost of overheads is deducted from the gross profit including wages and running costs. Then loan repayments, interest and tax are deducted.

◆ TIP ◆

Ask yourself the following after calculating the recipe costs and menu prices: can the market withstand my pricing? What is the competition like?

But first, you will need to price items. Get price lists from wholesale companies, retail shops, farm shops, specialist mail order food companies and other sources such as van drivers delivering produce in the area.

When starting your business, a degree of wastage (too much bread or salad is bought, for example) will have an impact on your GP margins but this will be resolved in time once the business gets going with good management practices. Buy the food when you have secured your first customers; then you will feel confident enough to have some non-perishable stock onsite.

How much to charge

When making an estimate, take into consideration the following:

Raw materials. Make notes of what every item costs from the pepper, salt, oil, butter and other basics such as flour to the main ingredients. Add the presentation costs too (herbs and anything else you may wish to accentuate the food).

Overheads. These are rent, insurance, taxes, water, gas, electricity, cleaning materials, employee time taken to help with the food preparation and any other expenses such as paper napkins, cocktail sticks, rubbish bags. When starting up, this may not be an exact science. After a period of trading, you may be more exact by adding up these expenses to find out what you will add to each catering job. As a rule of thumb, you should be looking for at least 35 per cent profit.

Simplicity. Don't make life difficult for yourself by devising complicated menus and time-consuming dishes; your own 'wage' will be small. Don't go for labour-intensive food if you value your sanity, especially if you run a busy catering business. You won't be able to fit all the work in.

Fresh ingredients. More and more, clients are looking for simplicity, quality and good food sourcing and won't be tempted by cheap food disguised by a blanket of sauce and poorly presented.

Amount. If you are catering for a small party, you will make less profit unless you charge more. Common sense, naturally. For a larger party, over 50, for example, the price can be reduced. Charge according to the time of year too. If you have little business in some periods of the year and are keen to get some to see you through a lean patch, you may wish to reduce your prices.

Invoice charges. Separate the charges for the food from the charges for equipment and staffing. You will be passing the latter on directly to the client and they should be itemised separately on the invoice unless you wish to include them. (See the example in Chapter 7 which shows an invoice with these included.)

Reception/buffet charges. If you give a list of canapés or buffet dishes to the client at an estimated price per head, price their choices and give an exact quotation. If you have only general prices they may unwittingly choose only the expensive items, leaving you with a diminished profit.

Your competitors. How much does a similar catering company charge? If you go for quality, you may find you have to charge more than your competitor(s) but make sure that you put in your sample menus what type of ingredients you use (free range, organic, locally sourced for example).

Value. Sell value, not price. If you want to stand out from the crowd, make sure your clients get their money's worth, and that they can trust you and rely on you. Offer services that other catering companies don't. Keep your premises clean, neat and hygienic and turn questions of price into answers reflecting value and quality.

◆ TIP ◆

If you are buying an existing business, approach the figures with caution. They may not always be as buoyant as they appear. Ask pertinent questions: is there wastage? Can I source my meat more cheaply (but just as good) elsewhere? Do I have too many staff? Do I really need printed menus or can I print off my own?

RAISING CAPITAL

Aim to raise more money than you need. You often have only one chance of raising money – it is very difficult to ask the same source a second time around for more funding. If your figures are too low your business proposition may not work long-term.

Work out exactly how much you need and for how long. Re-mortgaging your house (should you have the luxury of owning one) isn't suitable if you need money for the short-term. To cut equipment costs, consider renting and leasing options.

DEALING WITH BANKS

The competition between banks to do business with you can be buoyant so search for deals. But negotiate too. Stipulate your needs and suggest a rate of interest when you can start paying back the loan. It never hurts to ask.

◆ TIP ◆

You don't have to bank with the bank that gives you a loan. If the loan comes from a non-high street bank or is too far away from your business to pay money into, for example, bank elsewhere.

BUSINESS PARTNERSHIP

If you are going into business with a partner, or forming a company with investors or lenders, think about the following:

Choose your partners or investors with great care. Look for investors and/or partners who respect your strengths and weaknesses and vice versa. Clearly define areas of responsibility at the outset. These may shift as the business progresses so discuss these changes in full when they arise.

Aim for majority control with partners or investors as minor shareholders. But remember that you have to convince them that you are capable of running such a business.

Communication is all. Your partner(s) must, for example, be completely up to date with any transactions you may have made on behalf of the business.

Outline and protect personal investment as well as the agreed split of assets and liabilities. Get it down on paper and get a lawyer. (See legal tips in this chapter.)

CAPITAL EXPENDITURE

Note that this list may not fully apply if you are running a business from home.

The property:

◆ the property – its rent deposit and on-going rent or cost to buy;
◆ renovation and building costs including labour and materials;
◆ plumbing and electrical costs including labour and materials;
◆ toilet upgrade costs;
◆ floor covering, window blinds;
◆ lighting;
◆ heating, air conditioning, kitchen extractor fan;
◆ fire extinguishers.

Catering equipment:

◆ kitchen equipment large and small – from stoves to spoons (include rental equipment costs if leasing rather than buying);
◆ glass, cutlery, crockery;
◆ cleaning costs (including vacuum cleaners);
◆ rubbish removal costs;
◆ opening stocks: food, alcohol, cleaning materials;
◆ opening party costs (a good marketing launch pad for prospective clients).

Ancillary costs:

◆ telephones;
◆ gas and electric costs;
◆ office equipment;
◆ printing costs for menus, cards, publicity handouts, bill heads;
◆ advertising costs;
◆ promotional costs;
◆ graphic costs.

Accountancy and other costs including legal fees:

◆ accountant's and bookkeeper's fees;
◆ legal fees;
◆ rates;
◆ insurance;
◆ permits: fire, health, business licence;
◆ staff costs – waiting, kitchen, cleaning;
◆ breakages;
◆ contingency fund (for tax, emergencies).

NEXT STEPS IN FINDING FUNDING

It's time to persuade others to fund your venture with your business plan and capital costs worked out. The lender will want to see that the business will survive, so they can recoup the loan and the agreed interest.

You will need to satisfy the lender that your business has the right people running it and you have done good research into the projected customer base.

Tips for attracting financing

When you want to attract financing, it helps enormously to have the following well prepared and presented:

- sales goals;
- customer profiles;
- economic environment (slump or boom?);
- trends in the catering/food trade;
- competition;
- marketing strategy;
- key person resumés – you and your partner's strengths and background;
- your chef's background and expertise (if you have a chef on board);
- cash flow projection;
- revenue projections;
- taxes – VAT included;
- financing requirements: amount needed, detailed budget, repayment options;
- bank documents.

Tackling difficulties in raising finance

Even with a viable business proposition, it can be hard sometimes to persuade banks or other financial institutions to support your application. But do persist and if you are unsuccessful at first, try again. It may well help to revise your plan if necessary; take on board things that have come up in your discussions with the bank.

As well as banks, look at alternative sources of finance. Make sure you have applied for all the help that is available from government and other public sector organisations such as Business Link, the National Business Advice Service, The Enterprise Centre (www.enterprise-centre.co.uk) and other helpful institutions.

The Enterprise Centres, for example, will help. You can crystallise your ideas in confidence by bouncing them off someone who knows what it means to start a business. You can also get one-to-one advice on running and financing your business as well as technical, legislative and practical help, and join a range of start-up workshops, seminars and one-to-one advisory services.

You can also get step-by-step support on how to:

◆ put your business in action;
◆ research your ideas;
◆ plan your business;
◆ understand and plan finances;
◆ raise capital;
◆ understand and plan your marketing and sales;
◆ get your message across by marketing.

Business Link's 'No Nonsense Guide' is an invaluable tool with information on forming a business, sorting out your tax and national insurance, what VAT means to you, trading regulations, employees' rights and government advice and support. You can order a copy by phoning 0845 600 9006 or by going on the website www.businesslink.org.

BOOKKEEPING AND ACCOUNTANCY

It is essential to initiate good bookkeeping practices from the beginning of the business so that investors, accountants and the Inland Revenue can see at a glance the cash flow, expenses and profit and loss margins.

Record all your transactions on computer if possible (buy a computer software package) as this will give you immediate information on the operation: the sales, its mix (from different kinds of functions, other sales from conserves, cakes, for example), stock turnover and food and drink cost percentages.

Computers also offer a cost-effective way of reducing paperwork but if you prefer to hire a bookkeeper/accountant, add the cost of employing one into the capital costs.

Choose an accountant who has experience of the catering trade and a liking for it, and do a cash flow forecast together.

Bookkeeping and accountancy requirements

You will need:

◆ cash and bank records;
◆ weekly sales of all aspects of the business (e.g. food and alcohol sales);
◆ weekly payments (suppliers, wages, rent etc).

Record the weekly income and expenditure on print-outs or summary sheets so that management can see at a glance where the money is going out and coming in.

The accountant will also require information regarding VAT, sales, wages, purchases, operating costs (rent, rates, utilities, telephone, laundry for example), drawings for investors and owners and capital costs (maintenance, repairs, improvements).

This analysis of breaking down the business into the sum of its parts can be of immense help to see where the business is going, its strengths and weaknesses, its seasonal swings. For example, are you spending too much on laundry or petrol, and can these be reduced?

It can also be helpful in combating fraud and theft. If you see higher than usual meat bills but know you haven't been catering for large quantities, it needs to be investigated.

At the end of the financial year (31 March), two summaries need to be prepared: the trading profit and loss accounts showing the gross profit and the net profit and the balance sheet showing the company's financial position. The latter shows the assets owned and the debts owed. The difference between the two is the capital value of the business, representing the capital invested by the owner/investors and the retained profits.

VAT

Value Added Tax (VAT) is a tax charged on most business transactions made in the UK or the Isle of Man. VAT is also charged on goods and some services imported from places outside the European Union and on goods and some services coming into the UK from the other EU countries.

All goods and services that are VAT rated are called 'taxable supplies'. You must charge VAT on your taxable supplies from the date you first need to be registered. The value of these supplies is called your 'taxable turnover'.

You must register for VAT if your taxable turnover, the amount going through the business, not just your profit, goes over a certain limit. The current VAT registration threshold is £60,000 but you can opt to register for VAT if your taxable turnover is less than this if what you do counts as a business for VAT purposes.

The benefits for registration under the limit include increased credibility for your business but once you are registered, you will have to account for ouput tax on all your taxable supplies which are not zero rated.

You will also have to send in VAT returns regularly and keep proper records and accounts so that VAT officers can examine them if necessary.

There are currently three rates of VAT:

◆ 17.5 per cent – standard-rated supplies on most goods and services.
◆ 5 per cent – reduced-rate supplies on fuel and power used in the home and by charities.
◆ 0 per cent – zero-rated supplies which are non-chargeable. Examples are most food, books, newspapers and children's clothing.

For small businesses, there are a number of simplified arrangements to make VAT accounting easier:

Cash accounting: If your taxable turnover is under £600,000 a year you can arrange to account to Customs for VAT on the basis of cash received and paid rather than the invoice date or time of supply. This means that you are not paying tax on unpaid invoices.

Annual accounting: If your turnover is under £66,000 a year you can join the annual accounting scheme and send in just one return a year rather than quarterly returns most businesses do.

Bad debt relief: If you supply goods or services to a customer but you are not paid, you may be able to claim relief from VAT on the debts.

Flat rate scheme: You may be eligible if your turnover is under £150,000. It helps save on administration due to not accounting internally for VAT on each individual 'in and out'. Payment is over a set percentage of the total turnover.

Ten top tips for simplifying VAT for small businesses

1. Registering for VAT will change your pricing structure so always calculate these into any costings.

2. Apply to register in plenty of time so that you get the help available to you, your number in good time for printing onto cards, invoices etc, and for other purposes.

3. Be clear about the impact of VAT on your growing business turnover. Make sure you put aside funding to pay the VAT.

4. Good bookkeeping is vital for overall business management. Check the invoices you receive. You must have a VAT invoice to claim back VAT. Remember that a statement is not a proper invoice.

5. Always enter cash receipts in your books before using the cash to make purchases.

6. Many businesses take advantage of the VAT they've collected, making it work for them before being paid to customs. Pay the VAT into a separate bank account to accumulate interest. (Be sure to keep the VAT collections for payment only to Customs and Excise and not for other purposes.)

7. If you find yourself unable to send your VAT return or cheque on time call Customs on 0845 010 9000 and tell them why.

8. Consider making a part payment to reduce the surcharge (penalty for not paying the total amount) payment.

9. Always quote your VAT number on correspondence or delays/confusion will occur.

10. If you are not sure, ask. It's in both your and Customs and Excise's interests. If in doubt, shout!

PAYROLL

You need to keep records of all your staff, both full and part-time. Avoid the temptation to pay cash for labour which you don't record as penalties for income fraud are severe. You will need the following records for each employee:

◆ name and address;
◆ tax code and national insurance number.

INSURANCE

You must be insured, and it's not cheap, so take time to find the right deal. Do spend time and effort talking to the right insurers – i.e. those dealing in catering/restaurant businesses – and getting several quotes. Or get in touch with an insurance broker. Ask those who are in the catering business who they recommend.

Your business needs insurance for building and contents. It also needs liability cover for any litigation (such as a dispute or lawsuit brought against the business). Even if you are able to cover the costs of replacement or repair, or any loss that may occur such as a shelf giving way with a hundred plates tumbling to the floor, it would be irresponsible not to be insured against any problems regarding clients' legal actions.

Your biggest risk may be from guests at functions and staff – with items being broken or simply taken. It is also possible that someone might fall in your premises – a staff member or visiting client. The building itself also needs monitoring for safety.

Your policy must include fire, storm, tempest (however ancient this terminology is), burglary, malicious damage, glass and other covers.

Additional cover you may wish to consider is business interruption, which replaces lost income in the event of a claim where your business is interrupted. This could be, for example, because of physical damage to your property. Be aware that if your business is your sole income, bills need to be paid regardless of an interruption to your business. Do ask for cover which guarantees you payment on a weekly basis for cash flow purposes and not payment once the claim is known some months after the event.

Payments should be made until normal business can proceed and you have regained the income you would normally expect. These are based on last year's figures for the time of year and not necessarily during your busiest period. Even when the work to repair or replace is complete, it should pay on a descending scale until your business returns to normal.

Insurance details to look out for

Duty of disclosure. This means that you give the insurance company all the information they need, and is vitally important when confirming and agreeing to the conditions of the policy. The insurer must know what you wish to cover as your policy must be an accurate reflection of your business. Be clear and specific and ask for written confirmation in all areas of your cover.

Public liability. This covers injury and property damage caused by your personal negligence and/or business negligence.

Product liability. This relates to any products you provide, but specifically to food you serve, either bought-in or food cooked on the premises. Should a customer find a nail in a roll (yes, it happened to me), you are liable.

Manager liability. This covers you for staff looking after customers in the absence of the owner. Customers, when in sueing mood, will not only sue you and your business but also the staff representing you at the time.

◆ TIP ◆

If you have a personal accident and sickness/income policy it is advisable to continue with this.

Fraud and theft in the catering business

Look out for the following:

◆ stock sold for cash;
◆ selling stock to other businesses;
◆ use of stolen credit cards;
◆ suppliers adding the date into the total, short-weighing, overcharging;
◆ suppliers delivering short orders and charging for complete orders;
◆ theft of food, drink, equipment, money by staff.

CREDIT/DEBIT CARDS

If you set up a mail order business for your produce, or supply businesses on a regular basis, this will apply to you. In today's market, card payment is the preferred method of payment; more than half of all adults regularly make debit card purchases. However, this is not the usual method of payment for the catering industry, especially the small end of the scale so it may not be applicable to you.

There are lots of benefits when customers pay by credit/debit card including:

◆ no cash restrictions can mean that customers spend more which means an increased turnover and profit;
◆ part of your banking becomes automated, making procedures simpler and faster.

Contact Visa or other credit or debit card companies to find out how to set up card payments. Negotiate charges with the card companies and renegotiate those charges a year after trading as they may see a good, profitable company in the making and wish to partake in your success long-term.

TOP LEGAL TIPS

Put it in writing

Do put all your business deals and agreements in writing. If you have a verbal agreement get confirmation in writing as a verbal one is often difficult to put into effect if problems arise. A written record will also prevent people from trying to change their minds or giving you a different story at a later stage.

It pays to get advice early on

Get legal advice early on when renting or buying a property or setting up a partnership as it will pay in the long run. Problems can arise in the long-term if this is neglected. Ask for an estimate of the cost if you seek a lawyer's advice.

Get someone to recommend a solicitor

Solicitors specialise in many areas of the law, so this can be a daunting step. Recommendations from other companies is a good start. Do ask solicitors for testimonials and references and follow these up.

Keep up to date with changes in the law

Employment law is constantly changing so do keep up to date by contacting your local job centre. Every employer must provide a statement of employment clearly laying down certain details. It can be in your interests to include policies that are not needed by law to safeguard you. For example, the kind of meals you will provide for your staff and what kind of dress code is suitable.

AVOIDING DEBT

Even if you have good finance and accountancy practices, there may be worrying times when some good, practical advice from experts would help enormously. Sometimes the psychological boost of just talking to someone who deals with financial problems is quite energising.

The Business Debtline (0800 197 6026) is a national telephone service that offers free, confidential and independent advice to small businesses on tackling cashflow problems by:

- preparing a budget for your business;
- prioritising all your debts;
- dealing with court proceedings;
- understanding bankruptcy;
- avoiding repossession of your home and business;
- dealing with tax matters;
- negotiating with creditors and bailiffs and dealing with most other debt and cashflow issues that you and your business may face.

PROFESSIONAL ADVICE

The Federation of Small Businesses (FSB) is the leading organisation for small businesses in the UK and campaigns on their behalf to improve the financial and economic environment in which they operate. Alongside this influential lobbying, FSB members also enjoy a unique protection and benefits package providing instant access to legal and professional advice and support. For further details visit their website: www.fsb.org.uk.

There are other useful contacts that can help you make the right business decisions.

The Small Business Service (SBS) operates a number of schemes and initiatives that are designed to help small businesses in a variety of ways. They encourage businesses to be more innovative and to exploit new technologies, help get finance more readily and can provide ways for businesses to measure and improve efficiency. Their website is www.business.link.gov.uk.

The SBS also oversees the work of the network of local Business Link offices that operate throughout England. Similar services for lowland Scotland are Business Gateway, Business Information Source in Highland Scotland, Business Connect in Wales and the Local Economic Development Unit for Northern Ireland.

Business Links provide independent and impartial advice, information and a range of services to help small firms and those starting up new businesses. Call Business Link on (0845 600 9006).

The Enterprise Centre 'enabling businesses to start, survive and succeed' provides Business Link services by offering start-up workshops, seminars on taxation, marketing, bookkeeping and other useful help. www.enterprise-centre.co.uk or info@enterprise-centre.co.uk.

The British Chamber of Commerce (BCC) is the national face of the UK's network of accredited Chambers of Commerce and campaigns to reduce burdens on business and create a more favourable business environment. For further help contact the BCC's website: www.britishchambers.org.uk.

USEFUL CONTACTS

◆ Better Payment Practice Group
For advice on getting paid on time and guidance on late payment legislation:
www.payontime.co.uk

◆ British Insurance Brokers Association
020 7623 9043
www.biba.org.uk

◆ Valuation Office Agency
Information on non-domestic rates payable on business premises.
020 7506 1700
www.voa.gov.uk

◆ Career Development Loans
Deferred payment loans from £300 to £8,000: 0800 585 505.
www.lifelonglearning.co.uk

◆ National Business Angels Network
Information on development finance: 020 7329 2929.
www.bestmatch.co.uk
Or Community Development Finance Association: 020 7357 7356.
www.cdfa.org.uk

◆ Employment Tribunal Service
Details of what to do if you're taken to an employment tribunal:
0845 795 9775.

◆ Federation of Small Businesses
01253 336000.
www.fsb.org.uk

◆ Finance and Leasing Association
Find out more about business asset finance: 0208 7836 6511.
www.fla.org.uk

◆ Health and Safety Executive
Information on health and safety rules for small businesses; free leaflets.
HSE infoline: 08701 545500.
www.hse.gov.uk

◆ Inland Revenue Helpline for the Newly Self-Employed
To register as self-employed if you're going into business as a sole trader
or partnership: 08459 15 45 15.
www.inlandrevenue.gov.uk

◆ Inland Revenue Self-Assessment Orderline
Forms, leaflets and factsheets on self-assessment: 0845 9000 404.

◆ Jobcentre Plus
They can help you find the right person for your business: 0845 601 2001.
www.jobcentreplus.gov.uk

◆ National Federation of Enterprise Agencies
01234 354055.
www.nfea.com

◆ Small Firms Loan Guarantee
Government scheme guaranteeing loans for firms which can't get bank finance because of a lack of security: 0114 2597308.
www.sbs.gov.uk

◆ Trade associations
Search for a trade association in your sector: www.taforum.org.

◆ Trading Standards Institute
0970 872 9008.
www.tradingstandards.gov.uk

6

Marketing Your Business

Marketing is one of the most important aspects of your business to get right. You need to give a clear, concise message. It also pays to keep on examining your strategies and to re-evaluate your marketing strengths – and weaknesses – regularly.

MAKING MARKETING A PRIORITY

The market is steadily becoming more sophisticated and the numbers of good catering companies to choose from are on the increase. You need to stand out from the crowd. It isn't enough to sit back and think that your good cooking will pull customers in without some extensive marketing on your part. This is where caterers can become unstuck. Get a strategy, allocate funding and do your homework.

You may find your time taken up with just running your new business once you are up and running. If you are the sole person the business relies on you to shop, cook, deliver, wash up, do the banking, the invoices, the cleaning, hiring staff and dealing with clients. It can be very hard but you will have to carry on selling your business to prospective clients to increase your client base – so do factor in time to do this.

If you are a one-man band with few competitors in a less populated area you may be able to spend less time spent on marketing. Your business will build via word of mouth and repeat business – but you have to do the leg work in order to get those clients in the first place.

This chapter covers:

◆ identifying your market;
◆ choosing a name;
◆ advice on signage;
◆ business cards;
◆ stationery;
◆ menu design;
◆ web pages;
◆ advertising;
◆ launching yourself in the market;
◆ getting a media profile;
◆ expansion of the business through cookery classes and cookbooks.

IDENTIFYING YOUR TARGET MARKET

This is vital. You need to identify your customers' ages, incomes and occupations. Perhaps there are some local businesses too? Then think about your customers' needs – corporate functions, weddings, social events, farmers' markets, mail order etc.

What about the competition? Look at other local catering companies' strengths and their market share. Are there few catering businesses in the area? If so, examine why.

And finally think about trends which will affect your customer base –
lifestyle changes, population shifts, and new businesses requiring catering.

There are various ways to get this information including:

◆ the business section of a good local library;
◆ your local Business Link office;
◆ local commerce or traders' groups;
◆ professional market research services;
◆ talking to prospective customers, marquee companies and suppliers.

CHOOSING A NAME

How do you see your company? Mainly catering for weddings and other
special occasions; for the businesses in your area; or as a jack-of-all-trades
offering catering for all occasions? Perhaps you want a thriving sandwich
trade, delivering to shops, offices and other outlets.

◆ TIP ◆

Choosing a good name to support business is crucial. Avoid gimmicky names at all
costs if you want to have a reputation serving quality food and offering good, reliable service.

What messages are you sending out with names like Kwizeen, Grace and
Flavour, Fodder Mongers, Radish, Tasty Tucker and Lushous? I would
suggest not very professional ones. But it does depend on your market if
you decide to go for a name that may incur a wry smile, or if you choose
another which fits your aims and personality. Many caterers choose their
names (Elizabeth Dunant Catering Partnership for example), link up partners' names (Letheby & Christopher) or select an impersonal name
(Regency Catering, Portsmouth Outside Catering, Cucumber Catering,
Regal Caterers).

At the same time, you should avoid choosing bland a name that no one
remembers. Or a complicated, tongue-twisting one which you struggle
with when you answer the phone. Your company's name is a vital word-of-

mouth marketing tool, and you will not gain if customers can't pronounce the name to pass on to their friends and colleagues.

If you choose a very French, Italian or Indian name it will pigeonhole you. Potential customers may be put off by the narrow menu that the name suggests. And although your menu may be in a French, Italian or Indian vein when you start your business you may develop it to provide food from all over the world: don't be stuck with a name that restricts you. Of course, if you plan to stick to the offering the best in that genre, then no problem.

YOUR SIGNAGE

The sign you have outside your premises can have a huge impact on your business. It is vital to make first impressions count. Never skimp on a professional sign-maker's expertise and make your own signs unless you have the gift. If you come across an appealing sign in your area, find out from the business who the sign-maker is in order to contact them.

Choose an unfussy, readable font and match the design and font to your other promotional material. Match the sign to your building. If it's modern, do modern. If it's Georgian, avoid going Gothic. Keep it simple. Light the signs. Consider carefully the colour and lettering so that it creates the right impact and is easy to read. One poorly-made sign of dark red with black lettering in my area is illegible: the business has shot itself in the foot before even opening its doors.

Add the street number in lettering large enough to be seen by a passing car. Could your business benefit from several signs for customers approaching from more than one direction?

If you have a gate, fence or wall by the entry to your premises and use any of these to place your signs on, make sure that bushes and other foliage don't obstruct the signs.

◆ TIP ◆

Make sure that any sign is accepted by the council.

Contact your local authority for permission for signage and lighting prior to having the sign made. It may not be passed due to size, colour or lighting, so play safe and make sure you haven't wasted your money if the local authority says no to your signs.

PROMOTIONAL MATERIAL

Promotional material can include business cards, printed paper, flyers, menus, sample menus to take away, newsletter and web page. Depending on the type and size of business you may not need too much, but some things are necessities. Decide what is necessary for you. A small catering company may only need business cards and make their own menus and headed paper via a computer, for example.

When designing your material, take the following into account:

◆ Choose a font very carefully. A funky, angular one may look good but is difficult to read. A clean, simple one is approachable and inspires confidence. Choose the same font for all promotional material for consistency.
◆ Will you have a logo? If so, you could design it yourself although it is well worth paying a professional to come up with something simple and effective.

Business cards

Make your business cards stand out via design, and perhaps colour. Remember to include the name of your business (easy to forget!), address, complete telephone number, website (if applicable), perhaps bullet points of strengths (you specialise in Moroccan banquets, your canapés are simply sublime, you offer the full works – staff, flowers and equipment hire for business events).

Printed paper

This will be used for letters and notes. Have a heading, registered office (if applicable), address, telephone/fax, email, website and logo.

Compliment slips

These are handy for sending menus or confirmation of an event or other information by post, but they're but not essential for the small catering business. (Position the 'with compliments' carefully to give you room to write.)

Flyers

Flyers are useful for leaving information at various places, for handing out, and for passers-by to take away with them. Have all the relevant information (where, what, who) plus a sample menu and bullet points of strengths (see business cards) on the flyers. They can be A5 or compliment slip size.

Brochures

Brochures are an essential marketing tool for large catering companies. Wait until you have established yourself and know your market before your produce one. When you do, add photographs, sample menus and information, a map if you have dedicated premises and details of parking.

A big 'don't do' in my book is photographs of smiling people, usually models, who look like the cat's pyjamas as they gaze at one another over a perfectly groomed table awash with lobster tails and stemmed glasses. You wish your business to reflect your style but you don't want to alienate customers by inferring you only cater for models or a younger crowd, for example – or serve food that is not for them.

Menus

Keep the menus simple with the name, address and contact details as a heading. You can have your menu printed if it varies little or seasonally, or hand-written (clearly) or computer-printed if the menu is small and changes more regularly.

Thanks to computing skills, it is easy to create your menus and print them off on a when-needed basis. A dirty menu gives out the wrong impression immediately and may indicate a less than sparklingly clean, hygienic business.

Sample menus are an excellent marketing device. Don't forget to put the name of the business and other relevant information on these slips. Have these, flyers and business cards accessible if you are working from a dedicated space where customers visit to discuss their catering needs, and replenish regularly. (As a compulsive collector of menus and flyers I am surprised how often basic details – name, address, number, website, times of opening – are omitted; the information is useless.)

Newsletters

These are a great way to keep regular customers informed of local and calendar events, with suggestions of menus to match the event or time of year. Or you can offer a special menu such as one that ties in with a tight schedule, menu changes, new produce, a range of wines new to the list or a celebration of the first year of opening. They can be as personal or restrained as befits your market and can keep your business in your customers' thoughts – a mail out often results in new orders and enquiries.

Website

Customers are increasingly looking to the internet for information and having a website is a boon for business. It is relatively cheap and good for small businesses which have a minimal marketing budget.

The traffic to your site is dependent not only on the website address on your promotional materials but also via search engines which will make your marketing even more productive. Searchers will either have your website address or may key in one specific word or group of words such as 'caterers in Norwich'.

Research other people's websites and either design it yourself or choose a designer whose work appeals to you. Look at a variety of websites for design inspiration. Get several quotes before committing yourself. Ask about the success of the designer's work, for example how many hits the website attracts.

Include on your website:

◆ who to contact;
◆ what your business offers;

◆ sample menus for a variety of functions;
◆ a wine list (if applicable).

Keep it updated – either do the upkeep yourself or agree on a monthly/retainer fee with the web designer. Above all, keep it simple and easily navigable. A static website, i.e. one which doesn't change or isn't updated, can send out the wrong signals and can arguably be worse than no website at all as it may demonstrate a slack approach.

> **◆ TIP ◆**
>
> Don't try to make yourself look up to date by adding a sham website address to your promotional material. People will look for it and if it doesn't exist this will give a very bad impression.

Put yourself in the shoes of the potential customer. Is your website welcoming? Practical? Professional looking and geared towards the customers you would like to attract?

Photo album

Take photos and keep menus to put into a photo album to show perspective customers. This is a real bonus to your business as some customers don't have the ability to imagine what you are offering; pictures are a very effective way of showing what they can enjoy. Take photographs of the food, your staff, the layout of a buffet, smiling, contented customers (but do ask their permission first).

ADVERTISING

To advertise or not to advertise – in the local press or in appropriate national publications – that is the question.

In my experience as a restaurateur of a small, independent upmarket country restaurant, it simply doesn't pay to advertise. Nor as a caterer specialising in buffets and canapés. It is far more effective to use other ways to get your message across: via *Yellow Pages*, mail shots, a newsletter, handouts, website and the internet. Word of mouth is one of your most effective marketing tools. It has been estimated one satisfied customer will tell between five and ten people about you.

If you do decide to advertise, look carefully at your many local newspapers and magazines to see which of them target your audience. You can obtain a media profile from your local publications which will give you a lot of research information, although you should make sure it is up to date. Look at the website www.jicreg.co.uk (Joint Industry Committee for Regional Press Research), to gauge the readership statistics of the majority of UK newspapers.

Ask pertinent questions when contacting the advertising department:

◆ What is the circulation?
◆ What is the readership? Age groups, for example, and standard socio-economic categories:
   A = higher managerial, administrative or professional
   B = intermediate managerial, administrative or professional
   C1 = junior managerial, administrative or professional
   C2 = skilled manual workers
   D = semi and unskilled manual workers
   E = those at the lowest level of subsistence.
◆ What are the readers' shopping patterns? (Taking holidays abroad, buying new cars etc.)
◆ Is the newspaper bought or free?
◆ If it's a daily paper, what's the best day to place your ad? It might well be best placed on the entertainment page, for example, which comes out on Thursdays.
◆ What's the best section to place your ad? Always stipulate where you would like your ad (if it appears in an inappropriate page, ask for it to be reprinted at no charge).

Other ways of advertising – paid and free
◆ *Yellow Pages*;
◆ posters;
◆ local tourism publications;
◆ local parish magazines;

◆ direct mail;
◆ newsletters (promotions, seasonal information, menus, new chef);
◆ internet;
◆ brochures and programmes allied to sporting events such as Glorious Goodwood in Sussex. Some people look for private catering rather than having to cook for themselves or while on holiday in rented accommodation;
◆ brochures and programmes for festivals, theatres, art galleries, art house cinemas and the like carry adverts and might suit your target audience.

Advertising wording

Your advertisement is selling your business so it must:

◆ grab the reader's attention (a picture, a heading);
◆ stimulate interest (menu suggestions for a specific event such as an anniversary);
◆ plant the idea firmly in the head of the reader that what you are offering may be just what they are looking for (value for money or quality of food, the latter locally and well sourced, for example);
◆ be concise and give out the appropriate information (who you are, where you are, what you are offering, how you can be contacted).

At the same time, it's important to avoid some things:

◆ don't be pushy, arrogant or personal ('don't look any further…');
◆ don't brag ('we are by far the best caterers in the area');
◆ don't use flowery language ('a tian of Mediterranean vegetables perfumed by rose petals');
◆ don't contravene the Trades Descriptions Act by offering something you can't deliver ('we offer organic fresh salmon sourced from the Pacific Ocean').

Other advertising tips

◆ If you have taken over someone else's business there may be an existing advertising contract. Do re-evaluate this.

- When people contact you, ask them how they heard about your catering company and compile this information. It will to help you gauge the effectiveness of advertising, and word-of-mouth booking.
- Don't respond automatically to a cold call from a sales person offering advertising. They will always try to persuade you with a must-have special offer or deal. Either ignore the call as politely as possible or ask them to send you details and then check the publication to see if the expense is worthwhile.
- Do stick to your budget.

YOUR MEDIA PROFILE

What message do you wish to send out to the media (radio, television, the press) if you are keen to attract attention this way? Recognise what your unique strengths are and what you are offering the public – and the media who you would like to woo – before you can decide how to attract the media.

What is your style? Is it purely culinary? Based purely on the character of the owner and or chef? Ideally it's a mix. An independent caterer must find his or her own voice – and own style – to project and to sell to the media.

Before touting for new business via media coverage, you must believe in yourself and be committed to be able to offer what you say you can offer. Can you deliver the goods? What makes you unique? What makes people want to contact you? Tell them: no one does it quite like you do, hence the popularity of your company.

How to get media coverage
A good way to do this is to make news through people. For example:

- you have just taken on a high-profile chef or one with an interesting pedigree or background;
- your produce is sourced via an unusual producer or is unusual produce;
- you have changed from being a commercial city high-flyer, or nun, or you are first Jamaican to open a catering business in the area;
- your business has changed hands after 20 years in the hands of a much-loved character.

Top tips for getting media coverage

Do some research. Look at information about newspapers, magazines, radio and television at your local library. Ask the librarian for help. Also, consider reading/buying *The Guardian Media Guide*, a publication with yards of information as well as useful media guides, *Willings* and *Benn's*, which have a list of all publications and their particular interests and readership.

Make a media list. This should include local and national newspapers, magazines, local and national radio programmes, trade magazines with contact numbers and emails where possible.

Send a press release. First, phone to find out who to contact – get the correct spelling of their name and send them the press release (see below on how to write one) with a photograph of the chef, a dish, the new owner, for example. Be sure you send it to the right person – it is a waste of time and money if you don't find out as it will simply be tossed out.

◆ TIP ◆

Should you call after sending a press release? Journalists are incredibly busy and some find it distinctly irritating to be called. Others don't. If you decide to try it, call them within a week or ten days of sending the release. Be quick and to the point.

Get in touch with those who do interviews or have a magazine-style programme, to see if you can be interviewed. Send a press release and some background to your business to spark an interest first. You won't be paid for any interviews, but you may gain invaluable publicity. You could also offer to do a culinary phone-in, or a 'dish of the week' for example, to get regular exposure.

Writing a press release

Press releases can be an excellent tool for business promotion if they are properly written and presented. They are not a page-long ad, nor are they a novel. Neither are they a promotional piece full of detail. They are concise, to the point and newsworthy, and they tell a short story, or relate an event, with clarity.

Be sure to read the publication you are targeting carefully before sending the press release. Do some homework and visit the publication's website and look at the style, the content and, if possible, buy the publication. This will mean you will be able to understand the readers' needs and get a better response from your press release.

Write with the journalist in mind: he or she is not looking to buy your product or service but to fill a news need. So when you are writing, ask yourself the question, 'Why should readers of XYZ care?' rather than, 'What's in it for me?' Start with an underlined heading encapsulating your reasons for sending it. For example:

Tom Glanville, award-winning chef from The Savoy, to join The Catering Team, Bristol, as head chef

Then develop the press release with newsworthy items, such as what strengths Tom's culinary style and background will bring to the business. Include any further information: Tom may be hosting a sample menu tasting or a charity promotion, or offering cookery courses.

Finally, add any other details. For example: 'Note for editor: The Catering Team, owned and run by Jessica Yates, opened in 1999. For further information and for photography contact Jessica Yates' – with full contact details.

> ◆ TIP ◆
>
> Always send the press releases by post. If you send via email they can be ignored or deleted.

Golden rules of writing press releases

- ◆ Use headed paper with a contact name, address, phone, email.
- ◆ Put 'Press Release' at the top of the page.
- ◆ Make sure the date of the press release is prominently displayed.
- ◆ Then put 'for immediate publication' or 'embargoed to July xx' (if there is a reason for keeping the news until a later date) also at the top.

- Choose your font carefully. It must be easily readable and not quirky.
- Put the text in double spacing, or small paragraphs divided by a space.
- Keep it short. One page between 400 and 500 words.
- If you must go onto another page, don't use the back of the page but another page.
- Always finish with 'ENDS'.
- Re-read it at least twice for grammatical errors, and spelling and information mistakes. Ask someone else to read it too for a fresh look.

OTHER WAYS TO PUBLICISE YOUR BUSINESS

Keeping afloat in quiet times

Invariably, there will be times when you will find the market rather quiet. Everyone has a period when things are not so busy, especially after Christmas or the dark days of autumn or winter. In order to keep buoyant, you will have to do other things to keep the business going. Here are some examples, all of which you can use for publicity.

COOKERY CLASSES

Are you a good communicator? Then you can capitalise on your premises and your profession to create a series of cookery classes and/or demonstrations. They can be one-offs, individual days or over a couple of weeks.

What to do

Firstly, decide how you will run the class. For example, outline a day, four one-day consecutive weeks, or monthly set of classes for six or more paying students (it generally won't pay to have fewer) depending on your kitchen size and what you feel comfortable doing. Remember to design the classes carefully around your own prep time, leaving plenty of time to clear up, have some time off and prepare for a function.

Plan the cooking with a domestic kitchen in mind and don't use hard to find ingredients (see below for suggestions for types of classes). Don't be too technically advanced or you may lose your students. Have a member of staff in to wash up during the class and help prep before the students' arrival and put this cost into your budget.

Write to your customers via a newsletter, put up posters and distribute flyers in libraries, shops and elsewhere in your area. Include all the relevant information and contact details.

You can run various classes, for example, if you offer a one-day course:

◆ 9.30am: arrive, coffee and talk. 10am: start students cooking a two course meal (or whatever you have chosen to do). 12.30pm: lunch with a glass of wine. 2pm: discussion of cooking and Q&A. 3.30pm: departure with pack containing recipes, newsletter, public relations information (flyers, business card, menus, other classes).
◆ Or, 10am: arrival and coffee. 11am–12.30pm: demonstration. Glass of wine with food. 1.30pm: departure, with tips and recipe pack plus menu and public relations information (see above).
◆ Or you could do the demonstration at someone's home who has a large kitchen, the owner getting some friends together for the demonstration.

Types of classes

As I said above, the classes can be for a day, two–three days, weekly or even seasonal. And there is a huge variety of what you can offer. Here are some ideas:

◆ The basics: soups, breads, pates, roasts, simple desserts, jams, biscuits.
◆ Cooking for family and friends: simple oven dishes using chicken or pasta.
◆ Cooking lunch with your paying cooks from scratch and eating the meal with a good glass of wine.
◆ Food from another country: Morocco, Spain, Italy, France, Thailand, Mexico…each country covered in a series of hands-on cooking classes or demonstrations.
◆ Cooking with spices and chillies.
◆ Cooking with fish: learning how to skin and fillet fish, for example.
◆ Cooking with shellfish.
◆ Cooking with meat and game.
◆ Cooking with vegetables.
◆ Pasta day: learning how to make pasta and sauces.
◆ Men in the kitchen.

- Cooking for children, and with children.
- Entertaining at home.
- Vegetarian cooking.
- Tapas day.
- Simple starters.
- Party desserts, buffets, canapés.
- Christmas: how to get through it as the family cook.
- Demonstration masterclass.
- A local celebrity chef/food writer doing a demonstration.

The most popular cookery courses are Christmas, Men, Children and Entertaining, but other subjects can easily grab the imagination if presented well and clearly on paper.

Calculate your costs carefully before deciding on a price per person. Offer discounts for group bookings: for example, one comes free if he or she books six friends. You can also offer gift vouchers for classes and demonstrations.

Make sure your classes measure up to expectations, i.e. don't promise more than you can do. Ask your students to fill in a questionnaire before departure for feedback; you will be surprised how much good market research you can achieve.

ADULT EDUCATION CLASSES

Put your culinary skills to good use by teaching cookery at colleges in your area. This is one route for extra income that can be explored if a) you feel you have the ability to teach adults how to cook and b) it won't interfere with your business as it will mean commitment. Contact the head of the adult education department at your local college or colleges to tell them about yourself, and find out what's on offer.

I have taught at several colleges and find it very rewarding but somewhat frustrating as colleges sometimes do not have very workable, clean premises. Check out the kitchens thoroughly before committing yourself to a contract: are there enough stations (workplaces) for students? Enough usable pots, pans, ovens, sinks? Are they clean?

Student preparation

Make up a realistic list of types of dishes you could teach your students or choose from the list above. Keep it simple (unless you are teaching haute cuisine). Make a shopping list for your students to go with the recipes so that they can be fully prepared. Specify ingredients such as strong mature cheddar, large eggs, castor sugar, vanilla pod rather than cheddar, eggs, sugar, vanilla, for example.

Ask students to bring containers to take the prepared food home plus cling film and labels so that packing up at the end of each session goes smoothly and you're not hunting around for receptacles for that bouillabaisse, chicken with pancetta or tart tatin.

One advantage of teaching is that it is a great way to get your catering services known; some of your students may well ask you to quote for a family party, wedding, christening or funeral.

ONE-TO-ONE COOKERY CLASSES

You might well also be asked to give one-to-one lessons to clients and friends. Treat this opportunity as a professional gig and stipulate the hours and time. (Be strict about this as it's very easy to find yourself chatting well after the lesson should have finished. Your time is precious and it is your business.) Depending what suits you and the client, you can either cook at the client's home or in your kitchen. Don't be too over-ambitious in the number of dishes you can jointly prepare and give clear recipes to the student(s).

MASTERCLASSES

Masterclasses are demonstrations of cooking methods which elude the home cook. For example, sauce making, bread making or Thai cooking. You may be approached by a group of friends who would like you to demonstrate dishes to them. Or you may offer classes to clients or friends.

When you are giving a masterclass, it's a good idea to make clear beforehand what you are offering. Generally speaking, a masterclass isn't a full meal but a demonstration of how to prepare and cook. For example, Thai ingredients, with a tasting of what you have demonstrated.

The audience

Be very organised and have a step-by-step timetable either on paper or in your mind before embarking on a masterclass. Don't assume your audience knows a great deal about the subject, but don't be patronising. Find out about your audience beforehand: if they are sophisticated foodies, don't talk down to them. Do be prepared for questions and know about your subject whatever its simplicity or complexity.

If, for example, you were cooking with fish sauce, *nam pla*, you should be prepared for a question about how it is made (fermented salted shrimp or fish). If you were preparing skate, you could tell your audience how they could prepare it at home and give more information on how to grill, poach, how to cut the cartilages, and that it is best bought in winter months. Always have plenty of information ready about what goes well with what, and give the audience tips they will be able to use at home.

Have ingredients on show to pass around the room and to taste. It is a good idea to have someone to help you during the demonstration if you are dealing with a number of people.

Have plates, napkins and glasses to hand around as well as recipes and any marketing tools you have such as business cards and sample menus. You may be asked to quote for a party by someone attending at a later date, so don't miss out on this opportunity to market your abilities.

CHARITY FUNCTIONS

You may be asked to prepare food for a charity function. These can be a lot of fun, and are also a chance to get some publicity. You may meet an audience/possible clientele hitherto unknown to you – and you to them.

When I do charity functions, I ask for the cost of the food only and donate my time to the charity. Although if the function is a distance away, it's perfectly OK to ask for travelling costs.

Be sure to get all the information you need in plenty of time. The charity's committee, who you are dealing with, should know exactly what you are preparing for them and how much it will cost them. You should know how many you are catering for at least five days in advance. Make sure you have enough helpers on the day and that you are not doing it all on your own if it's a medium-sized or big function. But above all, see it as being part of the community you live in, and enjoy it!

PERSONAL CHEF

You may want to put an ad in the local paper offering your expertise as a personal chef. I have cooked for a number of years on an ad hoc basis for a ducal household and derive much pleasure from it as well as making part of my living from this. You may be replacing the chef during his or her absence (holiday, sickness, in between chefs) or asked to cook only for special occasions. You may also be asked to cook on a regular basis for a well-heeled household or business. If this type of work does appeal to you, you can combine it with your other catering work, or stick only to being a personal chef.

WRITING A COLUMN OR A COOKBOOK

These are two excellent means of maintaining your profile. However, you need to have the right skills and commitment. Do you have anything offbeat or unusual to offer? Can you write clearly, concisely and interestingly? Will your recipes be easy for the general public to use? Can you fit in writing as well as cooking and/or running a business?

Writing a column
If you are keen to do a column in the local press or on the radio, think about what you can offer. Have you got a good story to tell about your

business? For example, do you grow your own vegetables, herbs and salad and raise chickens for the pot, all in the back of beyond, and succeed? Do you have particular expertise with unusual puddings, are you a dab hand at terrines or have exotic culinary pizzazz? Perhaps you come from a family which has had chefs for generations.

Contact your local paper, magazine, radio station and talk to the features editor or programme producer about a column. Find out their name and write to them outlining what you have in mind.

Writing a cookbook

If you have an idea for a cookbook, do your research. Go to a good bookstore and look at the cookbooks on offer. Which books would you like to emulate and why? Get their publishers' names and contact the commissioning editor by name.

Write a one-page letter, outlining your book proposal in clear, concise language your culinary attributes and other background which may be of interest – but only if it is relevant. No need to add your five A levels, your prowess at mountain walking and your bookbinding course.

The Writer's Handbook (published by Macmillan: www.panmacmillan.com) is full of information about UK publishers, agents, national and regional newspapers. *The Guardian Media Guide* (Atlantic Books) is also useful.

Contact the Guild of Food Writers (www.gfw.co.uk) for advice how to become a member once you have burst into print.

It takes time and perseverance to get on this particular ladder (as I can testify) but dogged determination can pay off (as I can testify too!).

Do not take on too much media work (should you be so lucky!) – writing a column, a book, TV, radio – as it may take you away from those stoves for too long and your business will suffer. Working in the media is fun, but often fleeting.

FARMERS' MARKETS AND FOOD FESTIVALS

Having a stall (or sharing one) at your local and regional farmers' markets and food festivals is a great chance to sell your business. Have flyers, sample menus, cards and any other publicity materials ready to hand out. It is, of course, also a great place simply to sell your products. You can use the opportunity to really market your food well.

Put an easy-to-read list of your products in prominent places around the stall, highlighting your unique selling point (for example, organic/home-grown ingredients/an unusual ingredient/vegetarian/vegan/Thai/ eco-friendly fish).

Display your prices on your products. Passers-by make snap decisions and if they can't see any prices, they'll assume that you are expensive and walk on. People tend to be shy about asking, but if you are friendly and informative, they will approach you.

Explain your products. Sell, sell, sell, in an informed, non-aggressive way. Involve your potential customers – ask them to taste some of your products. Nothing sells more quickly than hot (temperature, not chilli factor hot), freshly prepared food. Explain what's in the food and what it goes with (if it's a relish, for example).

> **◆ TIP ◆**
>
> Look as if you are enjoying yourself! Smile! Some stallholders look terrified of their customers. You will miss a golden opportunity if you can't be comfortable with potential customers.

If you are trying to sell your catering to passers-by, have a small camping gas burner to cook something appealing to get the crowds over to you. The smell will attract them and, by offering a taste of something hot and handing out information about your business, you are making a great impression on them.

Label your produce well to include the ingredients, use-by date, your business name, address, telephone, website or email address so that buyers can place orders at a later date if they like the product.

7

Looking After Your Customers

We have already looked at what kind of business you can have, and how to attract customers. In this chapter, I will look at what the next steps are once you have been approached by a possible client. Included in this is how to follow up a client request, and how to come to a menu decision.

I will look in more detail at what a catering company can offer, sample menus, client contract, and payment. You alone know your strengths as a chef or cook, or the strengths of the people you employ. (It doesn't matter if you call yourself a chef or a cook. Those trained at catering colleges tend to prefer chef, others who haven't gone through formal training calling themselves cooks. Restaurant chefs come as both, trained or not. It's up to you.)

WHAT WILL YOUR CATERING COMPANY OFFER?

As a caterer you will be asked to quote for buffets, drinks parties, corporate events, weddings, christenings, anniversaries – all kinds of events.

In common with most caterers of any size, I have been involved in all these and other events: grand picnics, not so grand picnics; meals for open air opera and plays; a tycoon wanting smart in-travel catering when ferrying guests to the continent in his private jet; funerals; 100th birthday parties; charity events in marquees, fields, galleries, schools, theatres, cinemas, barns; theatre actors wanting after-play suppers to take home with them; photo shoot catering; sandwiches for newsagents; opening parties at art galleries and open air sculpture parks; presentations to departing mayors; a press party on a Thames river boat for returning Atlantic rowing heroes; an amateur orchestra's Christmas and 21st birthday parties; film festival catering; food demonstrations; stallholder at local events selling produce. Even cooking for building site workers.

In short, like the boy scouts, be prepared for everything and anything if you want your business and experience to grow and develop. But don't take everything on – be selective. The above list covers many years' work.

If your forte is in one particular field, such as making sandwiches, gourmet or standard ones, for businesses in your area, then go with what you are comfortable with. Or, if it is making cakes for cafes, restaurants, tea rooms or National Trust outlets for example, then trust your instincts. Be happy in what suits you. If, at some point you decide you to expand your horizons, make sure you can achieve what you promise or you could damage your reputation by promising too much and under-achieving.

PRICING YOUR CATERING SERVICES

What really matters are service, quality, attention to detail and hospitality. But pricing is vital, and needs to be thought out. When pricing, think:

◆ cost
◆ competition
◆ customer.

Cost

Calculate the cost of running your business, taking into account your start-up costs and the required sum it takes on a per month basis. That will give you a good picture but always cost in your time. You cost too.

Work out the food costs, the amount you will spend on paying staff and overheads. You may wish to add a little for marketing, or take away some of your profit to achieve your goal: getting that client.

Competition

Find out how much your competitors charge either with a call, obtaining details by post or fax, or visiting their website if they have one. But make sure that the prices you find reflect what you hope to achieve. For example, they may be cheaper but be of lower quality. The service may not be as good. Or perhaps they include fewer things in the price. Can you do better?

Remember that your customer will do the same research to make comparisons and find someone suitable for their event. You have to make sure you aren't pricing yourself out of the market or, indeed, selling yourself short.

Customer

It is advisable to work every quotation out separately once you have asked pertinent questions to find out clients' expectations, rather than having set prices as the cost of your ingredients might go up.

Discuss what the client is looking for to give you more of an idea what to charge. They may want sophisticated, or more basic, catering. If they want something simple, you can lower your prices if you are keen to get the business. Do bear in mind that if you do this and you get repeat business from the same source, it may be difficult to charge more in the future.

Make sure that your client will always get their money's worth, be it for fine catering, superb staff or other attributes. Always see the customer as

Price

an individual, not just a client. See the event from their point of view and you will have a much better idea of how to deal with them.

MEETING THE CLIENT

Meeting the client for the first time, after an initial phone call or whatever brought you together, is a crucial moment. You are selling yourself and your business so you must be prepared and make a good impression. I suggest you have a list of questions ready to help you get the basic information you need. But first ask when the party is. Does it clash with an existing one in your calendar?

Ask the client:

◆ Who the client is and reasons for the party.
◆ What they are expecting you to provide (you may have outlined some initial suggestions).
◆ Where they are having the event and what the catering facilities are at these premises.
◆ How many guests the client expects to invite.
◆ What the estimated budget per head is.

Where to meet

You can always carry on talking to your client via phone, email or letter, but the client may well suggest a meeting at the venue or his or her office or home.

If you have dedicated premises, you might meet there. If so, it's vital to make a good impression; the client is able to tell from your premises if you are the caterer for them so make sure you present your asset – your catering company – to good advantage. You will feel comfortable being on your home ground and you can impress upon the client that you are what they are looking for by showing them the kitchen, any photography of events, sample menus and a nibble or two of food to impress them.

◆ TIP ◆

It's always a good idea take a sample or two of food with you when meeting new clients at their home or business. It makes a great impression and wins them over to your high standards.

Meeting clients at your premises will save valuable time. But don't be too rigid about this as at some point you will want to see the where the party is being held to get a good grasp of what you can do; meeting a client there is a great chance to do this.

Sometimes it's not possible to meet the client face to face because they are too far away: you operate a business in Caterville where the party is to be held but the client is 100 miles away in Clientville.

I often get requests from people who don't live in the area for a quote. I go on the information given to me and the whole business transaction is done by letter, email or phone; the eventual meeting is on the day of the event only. These are usually contacts made by personal recommendation and there is a degree of trust already achieved with the client who passed on my details.

What to talk about

It's important to make sure that you and the client are talking the same language: are you the caterer for them and they the client for you? The client may assume you are able to do a party for 500 with all the bells and whistles just because you are a caterer. In reality, any number over 50 has you fearful of your sanity. Be up-front and realistic from the start otherwise you will be wasting yours and the client's valuable time. Your reputation could suffer as a result.

After the initial contact, when you have found out the basics, you will be in a position to prepare for the next meeting.

This meeting is to find out in more detail the likes and dislikes of the client regarding specific dishes if it is for a small dinner party or drinks party, for example. If it is for a larger function, find out what the expectations are – a two or three course buffet, one course a hot one, perhaps? – and have a list of possible dishes for the client to look at.

Other key points to discuss at this meeting:

◆ The time of the proposed meal.
◆ The service – will you be hiring staff or not? (If it's a small party you may be able to do it yourself or with one staff member.)
◆ The drinks – will you be quoting for wine, water, beer, coffee, tea or will the client be providing these? (Often, at small dinner and drinks parties, this will be organised by the client including glasses. But, for larger parties, this will be part of your profit. Insist upon this or add a corkage or handling charge.)
◆ Bar staff, if appropriate.
◆ Equipment hire and approximate costs (or will you be using their plates, glasses etc if it is a small dinner party?).
◆ Where the party is to be held. If it is at the client's house, look at the space in detail and at the kitchen, in particular the cooker, fridge space, cutlery, plates, glasses, serving dishes and counter top space. If the party is to be held at a village hall or elsewhere, inspect the premises as soon as possible so that you can write the details in your confirmation letter (are there enough cups, saucers, plates, tables etc at the venue? And don't forget to add the staff time for washing up all these items).

What to do next

After the meeting, confirm as soon as possible the arrangements – the time and date, the venue, the menu, how many guests, staff numbers, equipment – and a list of possible menus for the client to choose from.

If you have partners or chefs, discuss the outcome of the meeting with them and involve them in the choosing of the dishes and other requirements.

Contact the client to talk over the proposal. Confirm the menu and arrangements in writing, including what deposit you require and when the final payment should be made. This may be altered by the client; if so, re-confirm what has been agreed in writing. Finally, when the client has agreed to the arrangements, remind, if necessary, for a deposit to be sent.

Every meeting with clients won't result in business. Nor will every quote you send out. Contact them several days after sending out a quote to make sure they received it and to see if there are any queries. A friendly call can make all the difference if the client has some reservations.

THE RIGHT KIND OF CLIENTS FOR YOUR BUSINESS

It is very tempting for the new businessman or woman to take all the business that comes their way. But not only do you have to handle the workload, you must also be able to handle the clients. There is nothing more disheartening that working at cross purposes with an impossible client or one who believes they know more about the business than you do.

Sometimes you need to make allowances for them. Perhaps they feel out of their depth in dealing with food, or nervous that they will be blamed if the right caterer isn't chosen. With a professional approach you may be able to win them over and establish a good relationship where they trust you.

◆ TIP ◆

If you feel you have met your match with a particularly difficult client you feel you just won't be able to work with, politely withdraw from any further negotiation and explain that you are not the right caterer for their event.

When dealing with prospective clients over the phone be as professional as possible, even if you are unable to satisfy their questions instantly. They may want to know what a three-course meal, or an entire wedding, would cost. The latter, of course, is an impossibility to tell them without some facts. Have information by the phone so that you can give them an approximate figures – for example, 'our buffet menus start at £00 per head' – but get it across to the caller that your menus are tailor made to suit the client, and suggest you meet to discuss the party's requirements.

Be aware of time-wasters and dreamers. You will be able to spot them without too much trouble; alarm bells will go off in your head quite quickly during a phone call. And if that deposit is not forthcoming as promised and as set out in a letter of confirmation, it may well be a sign that they have no intention of sticking to the rules. They may even try to get you to lower your prices in order to get the business. You really don't want to have clients like these.

SAMPLE LETTER AND PROPOSAL

The sample on pages 119–125 is a formal response to a client from a medium to large catering company. You may not wish to go through all these formalities but pick and choose from the format. If you are a one-man band, you may feel uncomfortable about this format, in which case, outline the quote simply and clearly.

For example, when I write to a client for a small party, I usually:

- outline the event – where, when, how many, what time;
- suggest three or four menus to choose from which can be mixed and matched as wished by the client (but check on the balance of the courses before agreeing to the menu – you don't want three courses containing pastry!);
- stipulate the staff per hour costs and any travel costs involved if outside a 20 mile radius;
- leave the wine up to the client. I don't charge corkage unless it is a large party. I may supply the wine too for these events plus water and ice;
- charge extra for coffee and tea and any homemade truffles;
- stipulate payment terms;
- ask to contact the marquee company if the client is organising a marquee to check on arrangements including the catering space.

You may also wish to support your company's worth by suggesting to new clients that they contact existing ones to check on your standards. I do this and, of course, choose clients I have known for a time and who are delighted with my services! Supply two names, phone numbers and/or email addresses.

Letter

Capital Catering
Mango Mews
London SW3 4JN
020 7432 1010
carol@capitalcatering.com

Ref. Private/Lewis 1/06

9 September 200X

Mrs Lulu Lewis
100 Alexander Gardens
London
N1 2BJ

Dear Mrs Lewis

Further to your enquiry, I have great pleasure in enclosing our initial proposals for the 10th Anniversary Celebrations you are organising on 14
November 2006 for approximately 100 guests for Lunch at 12.30 for 1pm at
100 Alexander Gardens.

The proposal includes some menus and details with pricing for your event
and I would be delighted to meet you to plan the party in detail.

I do hope that we will have the opportunity to cater for your event and I
look forward to discussing our proposals with you in greater detail.

Please do not hesitate to contact me if you require any other information.

Yours sincerely

Carol Godsmark
Chef/manager
Capital Catering

Encl.

Proposal

Catering Proposal for
Mrs Lulu Lewis
100 Alexander Gardens
London N1 2JB

Ref private/Lewis 1/06
10th anniversary celebration lunch
at 100 Alexander Avenue, London
14 November 200X

Dear Mrs Lewis

We are delighted to be considered for your event. In the next few pages
we have set out our initial proposals which I hope you will find match
your requirements.

Our aim is to provide the highest standard of food and service tailored to
your exact requirements. At this stage we outline budgets for all aspects of
your event but a lot of the detail has yet to be agreed. The menu prices are
fully inclusive of all the china, cutlery and cooking equipment as well as
the kitchen staff, management and service staff. There are no hidden
charges and in our total estimate we have tried to give you a clear indica-
tion of the likely cost of the event.

If you would like more information or if you would like us to come and see
you to discuss the event in more detail please call us. We would be
delighted to do so.

Carol Godsmark
Manuela Fwalty

Format

Your provisional times are as follows:

12.30pm drinks and canapés reception
1.30pm lunch is served
3.30pm speeches and prizes
4.45pm taxis

Menus

The food, cooked by Manuela Fwalty, is contemporary in style, combining the best ingredients and uncomplicated preparation. We recommend you allow a budget of £6–9 for canapés and £35–39 per person for a three course meal.

The price includes the following:

◆ catering management and service staff;
◆ chef and kitchen equipment;
◆ canapé presentation plates;
◆ Villeroy & Boch china;
◆ glassware;
◆ fine quality cutlery.

The menu does not include:

◆ wines and soft drinks;
◆ furniture hire;
◆ linen hire;
◆ flowers;
◆ meals for your entertainers;
◆ VAT.

Tasting

We will arrange a tasting of your preferred menu so that you are completely happy with your final choice.

Management and staffing

Our manager will take full responsibility for the smooth running of your party ensuring every detail is arranged as you wish it to be. Our staff are there to provide attentive, discreet and smiling service and we understand that your requirement is to keep the occasion informal and friendly.

Wines and bar drinks

A list of wines we can supply is enclosed. Any of the drinks can be supplied on a consumption basis. The price includes glasses, ice, bins to chill wines and water.

We suggest you allow £12–14 per person for drink.

Wine service charge for your own drinks

If you would prefer to supply your own drinks, we would charge only a corkage charge on wines at £5 per bottle.

Furniture and linen hire

We will liaise with Plate Settings regarding the number of tables, chairs and table linen you may require, the initial cost to be discussed with you, the final invoice to come directly to you from Plate Settings.

Flowers

We work closely with a number of florists and would be pleased to arrange a full quotation for your event.

Optional extras

If you wish to enhance the look of your party, we can provide the following at an additional charge. Please ask for details.

These include:

- coloured glass liner plate;
- coloured glass water goblets;
- Villeroy & Boch presentation plates;
- cut crystal glassware;

- ◆ speciality linen – velvet, brocade, textured fabrics;
- ◆ chair covers;
- ◆ napkins tied with ribbon.

Marquee hire

I do hope that the Majestic Marquee Company have contacted you and have arranged a site visit.

Meals for entertainers

- ◆ Sandwiches and light refreshments @£9 per person.
- ◆ The same meal as guests but at a reduced rate of £5 per person.

Numbers

This estimate is based on 100 guests. If your numbers drop, our overheads do not reduce in the same proportion and therefore our menu prices will increase.

Once you confirm your booking, this is the number we will work on. Please notify us of any change in this number as soon as possible and at the latest by 5.30pm on 3 November 200X.

Availability of catering services

In order to maintain our high standards, we are careful to limit the amount of bookings we take on a specific date. We are pleased to confirm our availability for your event and we will hold a provisional booking for you for four weeks from the date of this proposal.

Terms of payment

Once you have confirmed your booking, we will require a deposit of 70 per cent of the total expected revenue. This is payable a minimum of six weeks before the event. The balance is due within two weeks of our invoice being presented.

Terms

We would like to draw your attention to the full Terms and Conditions detailed on this estimate under which we agree to provide catering services.

Total estimated costs

Please note that this is intended as a guide but the final bill will vary in accordance with final numbers, menus etc:

Pre-lunch canapés @ say £6 per person: £600
Menu, service and equipment @ say £35 per person: £3,500
Wine and drinks @ say £12 per person: £1,200
Speciality teas and coffees from Union Roast with
home-made truffles @ £2.50 per person: £250

TOTAL: £5,550
Subject to VAT.

This estimate does not include the marquee, chair, table and linen hire, additional meals for the entertainers or other peripherals including flowers.

Why people choose Capital Catering:

Value for money

We may not be the cheapest caterers but we offer the very highest quality service at a realistic, all-inclusive price.

No hidden extras

Our staff are paid for the event, and therefore, there is no overtime to be paid by you.

Menus

Menus are tailor made to suit your event. We will incorporate your ideas or style. All food is made on our premises. We don't buy in unless they are specialist ingredients.

Experience and commitment

Capital Catering has over eight years of experience of catering for special events. We buy only the best ingredients and source organic where possible. We are a private company and ensure that your party will receive the highest attention to detail and commitment on our part.

10th anniversary celebration party
14 November 200X

Menu notes and ideas

Pre-lunch canapés
Hot (H) and chilled (CH).
Served on square glass plates with small napkins handed to guests.

Salmon carpaccio on sour dough (CH)
Crostini of creamy scrambled eggs with caviar (CH)
Middle Eastern falafel with a tahini dip (H)
Tiny pitta pockets filled with aubergine puree and Greek salad (CH)
Chipolatas with a honey and mustard glaze (H)

Starter
Duck liver terrine served with a homemade chutney and toasted brioche
or
Crab phyllo parcels with a saffron sauce
or
Warm salad of pigeon, puy lentils, crispy bacon and herbs

Main Course
All main courses are served with appropriate vegetables.
Seared fillet of blackened salmon served on a celeriac and potato rosti, a rocket salad
and warm balsamic vinaigrette
or
Charcoal grilled lamb with warm cauliflower, chickpeas and preserved lemon salad
or
Fillet of Marches beef with a tarragon jus with ceps and pommes dauphinoise

Dessert
Chocolate mocha tart with espresso ice cream
or
Pineapple upside-down pudding with crème anglaise
or
Poached pear with vanilla and lemongrass with a pistachio parfait

Coffee and speciality teas

Capital Catering terms and conditions

Please read and understand the terms under which we agree to supply catering services. Confirmation of booking our services either in writing or verbally will be taken as acceptance of our quoted charges and these terms.

Numbers

The high quality of our catering depends on every event we undertake being separately planned, purchased and cooked. This does mean strict terms regarding numbers.

◆ All prices quoted are for a specific number of guests. When numbers drop, our overheads do not reduce proportionally and therefore our menu prices increase.
◆ We require confirmation of numbers on the Friday before the week of an event or for Monday and Tuesday functions on the Wednesday prior to the event.
◆ If the number of guests attending exceeds the numbers booked (and we are able to cater for them) we will charge for the greater number.
◆ If the number of guests attending is less than the number booked we will still charge the total number ordered.

Cancellation

When a date is booked we reserve staff and kitchen time for that function on that date and we will refuse other events which come in later. Therefore, cancellation charges are payable for any cancellation of a confirmed date. The minimum cancellation charge is 10 per cent. This will increase to 50 per cent within two weeks of the event and up to 100 per cent within the week.

Damage to property

1. If Capital Catering's property is wilfully or negligently damaged or stolen at a function, the replacement cost is payable by the client.
2. If we book a marquee or other property on behalf of the client, the responsibility of security or damage to property rests with the client.
3. If a client's property is wilfully or negligently damaged by Capital Catering, we will be responsible under our liability insurance.

Ingredients

Whilst every effort will be made to produce the exact agreed menus, we reserve the right to alter a particular ingredient if it is not available.

Food left over

It is not our policy to leave left-over food as it is never the same the day after. If, however, you wish us to leave the food, we can transfer it to your own dishes once the service staff have been fed.

Cleaning up

We always leave an event as neat and tidy as possible and we undertake to leave the kitchen as we found it. We will not, however, clean the function area but will leave it neat and tidy.

Rubbish will be left in neat bags for your dustmen to collect.

Payment

Deposit payments are required from all non-account clients. Payment of the final invoice is required within two weeks of the event.

INVOICES

Get the invoice out as quickly as possible after the event. How you choose to present it is dependent on your business size but do make it look professional – whether you have printed invoices or ones you have perfected on the word processor. If the look is professional, your business will look professional, and your creditors will take you more seriously.

Weekly invoices

Using a computer will make your invoices look professional. It may be a lot to ask if you're in the sandwich business, for example, and a sole trader whose time is taken up by preparing a great number of sandwiches on a daily basis. But it's well worth it. Keep a daily record, hand in a record (a copy made on the duplicate book you can buy in stationers' shops) of the number of sandwiches supplied to the outlet and submit your weekly invoice either printed on a computer or handwritten on headed paper.

The same principle applies to sole traders who may be supplying cakes, soup, pastries and other items. To safeguard your business, make sure that the copy you submit with your delivered order is handed to the right person so that there are no disputes when your customer pays the bill. If there is time, ask your customer to check over the order. Remember that if you're late with an order, this may not be possible as the outlet will be too busy to do this.

Sample invoice

Capital Catering Mango Mews London SW3 4JN
020 7432 1010
www.capitalcatering.com   carol@capitalcatering.com

(Your logo if you have one or a quote)

INVOICE

Client:
Mrs Lulu Lewis
100 Alexander Gardens
London N1 2BJ

Ref: Lewis/01/06

18 November 200X

For 10th Anniversary party celebrations on 14 November 200X

Pre-lunch canapés for 100 @ £7 per person:	£700
100 guests @ £35 per person	£3,500
(menu, service, equipment)	
50 bottles of wine @ £14 per bottle:	£700
40 bottles of water @ £2.50:	£100
100 coffee/tea with truffles @£2.50:	£250
Total:	£5,250
(If you charge VAT, add this amount here)	
Less 70% deposit:	£3,650
Total to pay:	£1,600

Please make cheques payable to Capital Catering by
2 December 200X.

It was our pleasure to cater for your event.

I always add a small handwritten note to the client with a word of thanks and to say what a pleasure it was to cater for their event. I also ask if every-thing was to their satisfaction even though I also asked this at the event itself before leaving.

If you haven't left cards with the client at the event, send some with the invoice. These may be passed on to guests who have been delighted with your catering and who will tuck the card away for future use.

POST-EVENT SUMMARY

After the event, take time to write down the plusses and minuses of every event so that you can learn and develop each area that you felt you didn't excel in. Keep records of each party for reference and develop your filing skills so that you can put your hands on the information quickly. How many staff did you have for that birthday party for 50? What did you pay them? Where did you source that simply stunning lamb from? How much did you pay for the ice and could you get a better deal elsewhere?

I keep a shopping list of ingredients and write down on cards the amount of couscous for 100 for example, the numbers of red peppers to roast to go with the couscous, how many red onions and so on so that I don't have to go through the whole procedure again when figuring out the next party's couscous. It saves a lot of time and you can estimate the cost of each dish very accurately and simply.

Make sure, after a party, that your client is happy with the outcome. Call them up within a few days to find out a) if they are content b) if the prop-erty was left as they would have wished c) if there is anything you need to do (you may have left something behind and wish to arrange a time for col-lection, for example). Show that you have their best interests at heart.

♦ TIP ♦

Communication is vital to your business, so keep the dialogue going.

8

Food and Drink

Now it's time to work out your catering plan and how to achieve this. You need to sort out in your mind, and on paper, what you will be able to offer your clients in the kitchen space you have, and the amount of time you will be able to commit to your business if you are running it from home.

You, of course, may have a fixed idea – the reason why you thought of being a caterer in the first place – how you wish to grab the attention of your possible clients. You may have been testing recipes and have a good source of cook and reference books to guide you. Or you may be starting from scratch and need to think through very carefully what you will offer.

This chapter covers:

◆ sample menu and recipe compilation;
◆ cost estimation;
◆ how to charge clients;
◆ how to deal with customers with unsuitable menu requests;
◆ special diets;
◆ when to prepare food for an event;
◆ how to calculate quantities of food and drink per person;
◆ how to set up a bar;
◆ table sizes and seating;
◆ points for working a successful buffet;
◆ buying wine.

WORKING OUT WHAT YOU CAN DO

Important questions to ask yourself:

◆ **How many people can I cater for in my kitchen if I am the sole cook?** If it's a small kitchen, you can possibly do small buffet and dinner parties as well as canapés.
◆ **What kind of menus can I realistically manage?** You might not have sufficient refrigeration for a lot of food, either for preparation or storage. In which case, offer more simple food. On the other hand, you might have a large dedicated kitchen to prepare enough food for a buffet for 250 and sit down dinners for 150.
◆ **How am I going to create menus for my clients?** Start writing down food you love cooking and then create balanced menus with a number of options which will fit into your style of cooking.
◆ **What kind of sample menus would be best to sell my business?** As many people have conservative tastes, it may be best to have several menus which are 'safe', and others which mirror your more eclectic style of cooking and produce choice.
◆ **What kind of kitchen space is available to me at the venue?** If the space is minimal, the chosen menu must reflect this.

I have given some possible replies, and more information follows. But some of these questions only you can assess as skills, knowledge, experience and your premises will differ. You may be a caterer already but wish to change the type of catering you offer. If you are a complete novice or one without too much experience, advice follows.

♦ TIP ♦

Ask yourself, if you are the chef/cook, what cooking strengths you have. What do you like cooking? Are you quick? Tidy? Efficient? Can you cope under pressure?

COMPILING A MENU

What you like to cook

My advice is to put on sample menus what you like to cook. It obviously has to be reasonably broad or else you will go out of business. What if you don't like cooking fish? Unless you have set yourself up as a vegetarian caterer, customers will be confused when they ask for whole cooked salmon, a delicate prawn starter, or a fish soup and, for example, you decline to give them a quote for these dishes. They will go elsewhere.

Keep up with trends

As one in three of us eats out once a week these days, one way to see what people like eating is to read as many restaurant menus as possible. The tendency to eat more light food is a trend. But do offer food that reflects your business, not just a copycat version of what everyone else does. Give your business your own stamp, your unique selling point.

Read food magazines, food articles in newspapers, leaf through new cookery books. Keep in touch, in other words, with what is happening in the food world.

Skills come gradually

Don't expect to be a skilled caterer from the start. It is not feasible, unless you have had a lot of experience cooking, to be a complete professional. Skills will come gradually and so will your knowledge of how to handle clients, what to put on your menus and what works in your kitchen.

Knowledge of ethnic ingredients

A cook's knowledge of ethnic ingredients and dishes also has to be taken into consideration. If you aren't keen on Indian food or uncertain about Thai or Japanese ingredients, it may be best to leave these out.

On the other hand, if you are a really keen cook who likes to rise to the challenge, then you will experiment perhaps by eating out in ethnic restaurants, talking to ethnic chefs, suppliers and friends who may come from or have lived in these countries, and trying out a variety of dishes to offer your clients.

But your heart has to be in it to succeed. It's not enough just getting by and hoping that it will be all right on the night. Under pressure at the venue, these dishes may fail miserably. So hone your skills before trying out any dishes unfamiliar to you on your clients.

SAMPLE MENUS

When compiling a sample menu for handouts or other forms of publicity, or a menu for clients, it should reflect your abilities but also what you can cope with, so don't get too ambitious and promise the earth. Unless you are an accomplished, experienced cook, it is best to compile a simple, small menu which you can easily fulfil. Otherwise, you will be disappointing the client and yourself, and repeat business will be a non-starter.

Canapé and buffet party

Below I have laid out possible sample menus that a small- to medium-sized catering business could suggest for a canapé and buffet party. The client should choose a selection of hot and cold food to suit the client and venue. It should be a balanced choice, i.e. not all pastry or all fish unless specifically wished for by the client.

Canapés: from £X per guest
Chicken liver, herb and brandy pate in a light pastry case
Chipolata sausages with a honey and mustard glaze
Crostini of creamy scrambled eggs with smoked haddock
Mini pizzas with mozzarella, tomato and black olives

Smoked salmon with home-made dill blinis and sour cream
Tandoori chicken with a cucumber and a yoghurt dip
Thai fishcakes with a soya and fresh ginger dipping sauce
Tiny pitta pockets filled with aubergine caviar and Greek salad

Buffet main courses: from £X per guest
Warm roasted red and yellow peppers with a mint couscous
Fresh and smoked salmon terrine with avocado
Cold sliced chicken breast with a pine nut, lime and mango salad
Cold marinated duck breast with warm puy lentil salad
Spicy tiger prawns served hot in a tomato relish
and served with sticky rice
Roast fillet of Welsh beef served cold and with a
horseradish mayonnaise sauce
Hot new potatoes with butter and seasalt and fresh herbs
Green salad with a Roquefort dressing
Moroccan carrot salad with herbs
Tomato salad with mozzarella, basil and extra virgin olive oil
Assorted breads

Buffet desserts: from £X per guest
All desserts are home made

Chocolate roulade with strawberries and clotted cream
Lemon tart with crème fraiche
Chocolate tart with crème fraiche
Plum and almond tartlets
Individual chocolate torte
Baby meringues dipped in chocolate and filled with crème Chantilly
Fruit salad to include mango, melon, strawberries in a Cointreau syrup
Assorted artisan cheeses

I usually charge per head for a buffet but it can be a per course charge, especially if it is a wedding and the cake is the star. This is up to the client, so it is worth suggesting a dessert for extra profit.

Coffee and tea are charged as extra per head and usually come with cream, milk, different sugars and well-sourced chocolates or small sweet pop-in-the-mouth offerings.

♦ TIP ♦

Before putting anything unusual on the sample menus such as venison, quail or seasonal fruits, make sure you can source them and that you know the going rate.

DIFFERENT DIETS

You will notice in the above sample menus that there is a good balance to suit all tastes including vegetarians, who often don't inform their hosts that they don't eat fish or meat. This can apply at large functions where the host or hostess will not know all their guests individually.

I always add several vegetarian dishes to any buffet menu as meat eaters enjoy this food too – and will help themselves to it – so you might as well incorporate this food into a menu. It is nigh on impossible to keep dishes back for individual tastes so make the selection as varied as possible – with the consent of the client, of course.

Do ask your client if there are any specific diets that need to be catered for. Vegan, coeliac or non-dairy are possibilities. I make up dishes for these specific diets and keep them apart from the rest of the food until those guests have been identified. That way they can feel part of the party rather than being sidelined. (See page 149 for more information on special diets.)

YOUR CLIENTS' EQUIPMENT

When agreeing to a menu with a client in a private home or a corporate business, make absolutely sure that there is the equipment you require to cook the menu. For example, you will be in deep trouble if you arrive at someone's home to find that there is only one Aga to cook dinner for 20. What you really needed were two separate ovens and six burners.

As cosy as Agas are for their owners, they cannot cope with a dinner party for 20 unless you are heating up a stew and have a cold starter and dessert. If you're preparing a three-course meal that requires the use of the oven for three separate dishes, you're not going to achieve what you promised. And those Agas do have a tendency to lose all their oven heat when you've got something bubbling away on the burner. Being a former Aga owner, I know their pitfalls.

If you arrive at a company's kitchen to find that there is minimal equipment, the microwave seen as the only necessity by the company, your idea of making a paella cooked on a gas burner rapidly goes out the window. In my naïve days, this happened to me. And if you are unfamiliar, as I was, with microwaves, it can be a steep learning curve. But, against all odds, the paella was achieved. A little late, however.

When the company client decides what they would like from your sample menu, ask pertinent questions: is there an oven to warm food up in and cook the potatoes, for example? Are there washing up facilities? Refrigeration? These will make a big difference as to what they can order from you. Any dairy-based food will need refrigeration as well as fish and meat unless you are serving the food immediately upon arrival, which isn't likely.

◆ TIP ◆

If possible, visit the client's home to see their equipment so you can gauge the kitchen's assets for yourself and plan the menu accordingly with your client.

DINNER PARTIES

When compiling sample menus for dinner parties, make sure that the balance is good. For example, you wouldn't want three courses all incorporating dairy food, or three heavy courses. Look too for texture and colour when devising menus.

Sample menus

Menu A: £X per guest

Crab soup with cream, saffron and leek

Beef fillet with Bearnaise sauce

Dauphinoise potatoes and assorted vegetables

Individual apple tarts with an apple sorbet

Menu B: £X per guest

Chicken liver terrine with a sesame ginger vinaigrette and toasted brioche

Salmon fillet with a dill beurre blanc sauce

Pommes parisienne and assorted vegetables

Honey ice cream with roasted figs

Menu C: £X per guest

Wild and cultivated mushroom soup

Boned quails (2) stuffed with wild rice and thyme

Celeriac and potato puree and assorted vegetables

Lemon tart with passion fruit ice cream

I always make sure that the vegetables suit the main course. It is very important to get this right as the colour and texture, as mentioned, play a part on the plate. For example, I wouldn't choose parsnips and beetroot for salmon however wonderful these vegetables are, because they are too strongly flavoured and are more suited to venison, pork, lamb or beef. I would suggest fine French beans, broccoli with almonds and new potatoes with butter and seasalt with the fish. But this is up for discussion with your client. Guide them, however, into marriages made in heaven.

KEEPING UP TO DATE

Menus written in French are very out of date. The Queen is seemingly the only hostess – bar some restaurants too – to prefer this archaic way of presenting the menu outside of French-speaking countries. Pourquoi? Traditions die hard. French is, of course, a glorious language, and France is still seen by many as home and originator of the finest cuisine. But as Britain, amongst other countries, is a multi-cultural society that latches on to many food cultures in the 21st century, it is old-fashioned and is seen by some as being desperately pretentious.

Keep up to date too with food expectations; lighter food is definitely preferred by clients. Duck a l'orange and veal sweetbreads may have been the fashion in times past but tastes have altered quite considerably. Although you should be prepared for some more set-in-their-ways clients who may find pleasure in offering these and other dishes to their guests. Be flexible.

There is nothing 'wrong' in offering tomato soup or prawn cocktail. But it has to be the best tomato soup made with terrific tomatoes and prawn cocktail made with tip-top non-woolly prawns with home-made sauce.

SOURCING YOUR INGREDIENTS

Increasingly, well-sourced ingredients are leading the way. Source that organic salmon, that free-range chicken and eggs, find those artisan cheeses for a good cheeseboard. And serve the best bread you can lay your hands on and not cheap supermarket mass-produced rolls for dinner parties. Obviously, if you are providing a sandwich service and if profits are slim, your choice may be limited. But there still is quality to be found – so seek it out.

Be prepared to break some rules. If you can't make the best bread, don't think you have to make it just to be able to say you make everything on the premises. If you can't cook something better than you can buy it, there is no point it cooking it. But do buy prudently, wisely and with your profits in mind.

THE SANDWICH AND SALAD TRADE

If your wish is to be in the sandwich business, what kind of sandwiches will you be offering? Upmarket or ordinary fill-em-up ones? Whatever kind, do try to entice your customers to try different ones. It will please them and be more pleasurable to you to be involved in more of a creative business. Make samples for them to taste. Market them well.

What about offering a sample tray to a business or two just before lunch when office staff are at their most hungry? They'll be won over if you make quality sandwiches. After all, this is a captive market. They have to eat every day and if you present them with tasty, good-looking food, then you stand a real chance of being their prime supplier.

Use different types of breads too, not just the cheapest white bread you can get. There are plenty of good-value, good-quality breads to be had so shop around and make your sandwich business more profitable too by adding value to your product – exciting bread, quality filler ingredients – so that you can charge more. Present them well too with smart labels.

More imaginative salads are flying off supermarket shelves thanks to a leaning towards healthier eating. Don't lose out on this lucrative business. They are easier to prepare than sandwiches once the initial buying and cooking has been done. Present these well too.

Some sandwich suggestions:

- roast beef with beetroot chutney;
- beef with tarragon mayonnaise and rocket;
- the best BLT (bacon, lettuce, tomato, mayo);
- butter-bean pate with roasted peppers and coriander;
- caesar salad in ciabatta;
- camembert with dates and grated apple;
- chicken with saffron mayo and red peppers;
- chicken satay;
- coronation chicken;
- cottage cheese with pineapple;
- creamy smoked mackerel and cucumber;
- egg mayonnaise with smoked salmon;
- feta cheese with olive paste (tapenade), cherry tomatoes and roasted red peppers;
- goat's cheese with French beans;
- ham, brie and baby spinach;
- herrings on rye with sour cream and chives;
- honey-roast ham with mango mustard;
- mozzarella on ciabatta with tomatoes, basil and olive oil;
- mushrooms fried in garlic with roquefort cheese in a baguette;
- oriental vegetables with black bean sauce;
- pear, stilton and bacon on walnut bread;
- prawn cocktail with cucumber;
- prawns with lime and coconut dressing;

◆ salmon, fresh, with mayonnaise and lemon with herbs;
◆ smoked mackerel with horseradish and apple;
◆ chorizo and marinated peppers;
◆ spinach and cream cheese;
◆ tomato with pesto and tuna.

Of course, good ham and excellent cheddar plus other favourites will never be knocked off the best-seller list.

Some salad suggestions:

◆ Caesar;
◆ coronation chicken;
◆ greek salad with feta and black olives;
◆ lentil and sausage;
◆ moroccan chick pea;
◆ moroccan couscous with lemon chicken;
◆ moroccan couscous with mint, tomato, and red pepper;
◆ Niçoise;
◆ pasta with roasted peppers and tuna;
◆ potato and smoked mackerel;
◆ roasted aubergine, mozzarella, tomato and pesto;
◆ roasted Mediterranean vegetables;
◆ roquefort and French beans with hazelnuts;
◆ salmon, fresh, with pasta and dill;
◆ spicy chicken with rice;
◆ white bean, tomato and herbs.

CLIENT WITH UNSUITABLE MENU REQUESTS

Occasionally, a client will come to you with a menu already in mind. Sometimes it will be inappropriate; there may be several reasons – the number of guests or the venue, the price per head impossible to achieve, the ingredients not in season or too expensive to buy out of season.

For example, if you are a small company, you simply cannot even begin to think of preparing a sautéed fish course for 100. The entire party would not receive their meal in time, the next course – which could be equally impossible to fulfil – delayed because you haven't been able to start on it due to the fish backlog.

Talking them round

Perhaps the client has got the wrong catering company. Or perhaps you can convince him/her of feasible alternatives, such as a plated charcuterie with terrific salads and breads followed by pre-prepared dishes such as chicken in a white wine, cream and herb sauce with a selection of roasted vegetables that just need careful re-heating? And with a cold dessert to follow, such as your excellent lemon tart with a raspberry sauce. Everything can run smoothly with this kind of menu and with client satisfaction guaranteed.

Explain to the client how it just isn't feasible to do certain dishes, and that the guests won't be relaxed if they have to wait a long time for their meal. If the client is amenable to suggestions and understands your explanations about the difficulty in adhering to his/her wishes, then you can proceed with other ideas. But do ask pertinent questions. Don't dismiss the client's wishes totally as there could be a compromise: a cold fish first course? Seasonal substitutes?

> **◆ TIP ◆**
>
> Remember to do your costing homework before agreeing to any menu changes and give it in writing to the client so that you both know where you stand when it comes to settling the bill.

RECIPES

Keep a full list of recipes of all the dishes on your menu and any others you may wish to incorporate into your business. It's a good idea to work out the costings per head and the amount you spend for future reference. Make sure it can be easily understood by other cooks who you may ask to prepare this particular dish. If the dish has a lot of seasonal ingredients, and, as such, is only possible to prepare at certain times of the year, make a note of it.

Do keep recipes even for the basics – mayonnaise, stocks, pastry dough, a marinade, a vinaigrette – in case you need to ask someone else to cook for you in an emergency or if you have taken on new staff. These recipes can be just a mere checklist of ingredients rather than the complete recipe. For example, you may wish to write down all the ingredients for a salsa – ripe tomatoes, spring onions, chillies, coriander, lime juice – to jog your memory.

Changing and adding recipes

Keep looking out for new recipes. You may be influenced by some of the more famous chefs in their newspaper or magazine columns, or cookbooks. Cookbooks of the past and family recipes are also good avenues of research. It could be just one ingredient that will inspire you to create a new dish for your repertoire.

Adapt recipes. There is no need to follow them to the last bunch of parsley or pinch of nutmeg. Don't forget, however, that there is little new under the sun. These cookbooks' recipes are often just adaptations of other recipes with maybe a subtle change of ingredients or name.

Keep ringing the changes when sending out sample menus to regular and prospective customers. It will keep you on your toes and will hopefully inspire the customer to employ you. Your changing recipe collection is a powerful marketing tool so use it to your advantage.

Don't become complacent. Keep re-inventing your business to make it vibrant and appealing to customer and staff alike. Anyone who keeps churning out the same old quiche recipe, for example, is either not a cook at heart or has lost interest in the business.

INSTRUCTING KITCHEN STAFF

The main cook is responsible for teaching staff how to cook recipes devised by him or her in an abbreviated, professional way. These recipes are a kind of shorthand, a checklist of ingredients and method, a variety of pointers rather than the usual recipe of full measurements found in cookbooks.

Develop a card system or file away recipes on a computer so that you can always find the required recipe at short notice to give it to a new chef who may not have cooked the dish before or is not familiar with your method.

Compile a master file in which each recipe is under headings such as soups (hot and cold), salads (warm and cold), chicken, fish, beef, lamb, liver and so on. For desserts you could have sub-headings such as ice creams, English puddings, fruit tarts, dairy desserts, pastries and basic preparations such as proper custard or chocolate sauce.

Add the date when the dish was on the menu, where the original recipe came from, its page if from a cookbook. Cross-indexing is also helpful, for example, lemon-based recipes.

Add notes to recipes too if they have been modified: the temperature needed to be changed, the type of chocolate giving the best results, how many servings each recipe yields.

◆ TIP ◆

For ease of teaching, stick to either the metric or imperial system. This will simplify the work in the kitchen.

Example of long recipe and its shortened version
Long recipe
Apple tart on puff pastry with a caramel sauce: for 2

4 Golden Delicious dessert apples, peeled, halved and cored
2 thin rounds of puff pastry 15cm in diameter and pricked with a fork to prevent rising
10g caster sugar
knob of butter
sugar syrup (see page 132 in *Divine Desserts*)
caramel sauce (see page 134 in *Divine Desserts*)

1. Pre-heat the oven to 170°C. Cut the apples into very thin slices and arrange around the pastry in a circle, starting at the edge and working towards the centre.

2. Sprinkle the apples with sugar then dot with the butter.

3. Place the tarts on a baking tray and bake for around 20–25 minutes or until the base is cooked and light brown. If the apples have not caramelised well place under a grill or salamander, covering the edges of the pastry so that they don't burn. Or use a blow torch.

4. Glaze with the sugar syrup and serve with several tablespoonfuls of caramel sauce.

Shortened version
Apple tart recipe: for 2

4 apples, peeled, cored and cut thinly
2 rounds of puff pastry
caster sugar
butter
sugar syrup (see recipe 132 in *Divine Desserts*)
caramel sauce (see recipe 134 in *Divine Desserts*)

Put apple slices on pastry in circles, sprinkle with sugar, add butter. Bake in 170 C oven until browned and caramelised. Continue with blow torch if necessary. Glaze with sugar syrup. Garnish with caramel sauce.

GUIDE TO FOOD QUANTITIES

Lunch and dinner parties

When calculating how much you will need to provide per person, dinner parties are straightforward if it is the tried and tested three course formula: one good ladleful of homemade soup, one chicken breast per person, vegetables to match, one slice of lemon tart, one or two scoops of home-made vanilla ice cream. Simple. You can do it with your eyes closed. For extra reassurance, look at the general measurement guide below.

Canapés

Choose food that will give a variety of texture, flavour and colour.

- For pre-dinner canapés with drinks: four per person.
- For a reception party lasting two hours: ten per person.
- For a wedding reception/event without a meal afterwards: 15 per person.
- You may wish to suggest to clients a mix of savoury and sweet for the wedding reception/event: 12 savoury and three sweet, for example.

Tips for serving canapés

- Have different types of serving dishes. Some canapés look terrific on glass, others on white china or multi-coloured dishes.
- Make canapés bite-sized.
- Avoid over-garnishing; it is not practical.
- Start with cold canapés and offer hot ones when the majority if not all guests have arrived.
- Offer small napkins with canapés.
- If using cocktails sticks make sure you take away the discarded ones so they are not used twice.
- Avoid using a cloth base on a serving dish – it may look fine the first time around but will soon look very messy.
- For a ritzy, wow look, place individual portions on Chinese china spoons, small spoons or forks or in shot glasses.
- You can never have enough chipolata sausages glazed with honey and Dijon mustard.

Drink quantities

- For a drinks party allow $\frac{1}{2}$ bottle of wine or sparkling wine or Champagne per person, $\frac{1}{2}$ litre of soft drink and mineral water per person.
- Allow two glasses per person (one for wine, one for water or soft drinks). People put their glass down too and pick up others from offered trays so it's best to have a good number.
- Pre-dinner: $\frac{1}{3}$ bottle per person.
- Dinner: $\frac{1}{2}$ bottle per person plus $\frac{1}{2}$ litre water per person.

Tips for the bar set-up

◆ Position the bar in a logical place so that it doesn't form a bottleneck, for example by the front door or between two adjoining rooms or in a narrow hall.

◆ Use full-length tablecloths over trestle tables or other rectangular tables as these are the most practical to use. If the cloth goes down to the ground, you can place bottles, glass boxes and other equipment on the floor that won't be seen.

◆ Have the following: corkscrew, bottle opener, cutting board and knife if making cocktails or slicing lemons or oranges for soft drinks, cloths for spillage and glass polishing, ice tongs or spoon, ice bucket.

◆ To cool wine at parties with limited or no refrigeration, use clean dustbins or large plastic bucket-like containers. Place a plastic bag or newspapers underneath to avoid the floor being damaged by condensation. Put ice in the bottom, add bottles and cover with ice.

◆ Dress the bins with cloths (an extra tablecloth?) if on view.

◆ If there is a shortage of ice, use part ice and part cold water.

◆ Chill the bottles a good two hours before service.

◆ If the drinks are on a sale and return basis, the labels must remain intact so don't chill all the bottles at once and only chill them when necessary.

◆ To make service quicker if there is limited time to get drinks served, loosen the foil on Champagne bottles and uncork wine bottles and replace the corks (it might be a little tight but it's manageable) halfway.

◆ Avoid using plastic glasses – they do terrible things to wine and most other drinks.

◆ Avoid using coloured glass – it changes the colour of the wine, making it look pretty dreadful.

Buffets

When calculating for a more adventurous buffet, look at the most popular dishes you have put on your own menu and double the amounts needed as you won't want to run out of these particular dishes. I have taken the chosen menu for the dishes listed under Buffet on page 132.

Remember: you will have asked your clients to choose a selection from the list, not the whole menu. When they have narrowed it down, for example to the salmon terrine, the chicken breast, the roast beef, potatoes, green salad, carrot salad, assorted breads, fruit salad and chocolate roulade, then calculate as follows.

Per person:

- 1 large slice of salmon terrine approximately 80–100g;
- 2 slices of chicken 80–100g;
- 2 slices of beef 100–150g (always popular);
- potatoes: 100g. Hot new potatoes with seasalt and butter are always popular. Or allow 5–6 new potatoes per person if you prefer this method;
- salad: 40–50 g;
- carrot salad: 100g;
- fruit: 100g prepared fruit;
- chocolate roulade: 1 large slice approximately 80–100g;
- several slices of bread, depending on the type of bread, per person.

Tips for the buffet service

- Place plates, cutlery and napkins at either end of the buffet tables to lessen the queue.
- Have several stations (several tables put together for food service) if the buffet party is a large one. This way, a mad scramble is averted.
- Communicate with guests where to go. They may just join a queue and not be aware that there is another station to go to so that they can be served more quickly. Or invite guests table by table to come to the buffet table to avoid queues.
- Replenish dishes quickly and tidily or have dishes in the prepping area ready to replace empty dishes.
- Tidy up the buffet table as service proceeds. There is nothing worse than later guests looking at a food bombsite. And if it's your host/ess who witnesses the mess, you won't be asked back.
- Make sure that all guests have had the main buffet food before offering seconds.
- If possible, place desserts at separate stations.
- If space permits, have coffee and tea at a separate station or clear the main buffet and lay out this service on the vacated space.
- Make sure that there is good space between buffet tables and guests' tables as there is plenty of movement by guests and staff, which may create a bottleneck.

General guide to quantities

This list can be applied to buffets, dinner parties, picnics or other forms of catering.

Meat: chicken, beef, lamb, pork, veal, duck, venison or other game

◆ 225g per person for roasting;
◆ 140g per person for stews and casseroles;
◆ 115g per person for a buffet, if serving other dishes such as fish;
◆ ribs: 3 per person;
◆ grouse or pigeon: 1 per person;
◆ quail: 2 per person as a main course or one as part of a buffet.

Fish and seafood

◆ 220g filleted fish per person for a main course;
◆ 115g per person for a buffet;
◆ 85–115g per person for a buffet is serving other dishes such as meat or poultry;
◆ lobster: whole for main course if small or half if large, half for first course;
◆ scallops: 4 large ones for main course, 2 large ones for a first course.

Vegetables and salad

◆ prepared vegetables: 115g per person if served with another vegetable;
◆ salad leaves (washed and picked over): 60g per person for a first course or buffet or 30g for a main course;
◆ potatoes: 180g per person (unpeeled weight);
◆ potatoes, new: 115g per person.

Rice, pasta and grains

◆ risotto rice: 45g per person for first course, 85g per main;
◆ rice, general: 30g per person with a main course or in a salad;

- dried beans, lentils, grains such as couscous: 60g per person with a main course or as part of a salad;
- pasta and noodles: 85g per person for a first course, 140g for a main course or 30g with a main course and 2 vegetables.

Dairy produce

- cheese: 115g per person as a separate course or half this if part of a buffet;
- butter: 30g if served with bread or with biscuits with cheese;
- cream or milk: 60ml per coffee or tea;
- cream for desserts: 85ml per person;
- ice cream: 50ml per person if with a dessert or 140ml for ice cream on its own.

Other

- small rolls: 1–2 per person;
- large rolls: 1 per person;
- bread: 2 slices per person;
- mousses, parfaits, terrines: 115g per person;
- fresh fruit salad: 115g per person;
- tart: a 30cm tart gives 10 portions;
- sauce: 60ml per person for a main course
- mayonnaise: 30ml per person;
- vinaigrette: 30 ml per person.

◆ TIP ◆

Always work in either metric or imperial for good results.

Getting the amounts right

When making couscous and carrot salad for a large party, for example, I generally measure out a portion using a standard-sized serving spoon, transferring each serving spoonful into another container and counting,

counting, counting. It's a safeguard to make sure there is sufficient food. This way, I don't prepare too much – or too little. But each caterer soon devises his or her own way to getting the amounts as right as possible.

It comes with practice and soon you'll be able to look at an amount of food and be able to calculate it accurately for the number of portions. And you will know by experience which are the most popular dishes you provide.

GUIDE TO TABLES, SEATING AND DANCE FLOOR SPACE

Table sizes and numbers
- 5 foot/1.5 metre round table: 8–10 guests
- 6 foot/1.8 metre round table: 10–12 guests
- 4 foot/1.2 metre x 8 ft/2.4 metre rectangular table: 12 guests
- 4 foot/1.2 metre x 10 ft/3 metre rectangular table: 14 guests
- 4 foot/1.2 metre x 12 ft/3.6 metre rectangular table: 16 guests

---

◆ TIP ◆

Use different kinds of tables to maximise the space. Rectangular ones take up more space than round ones.

Seating
- Afternoon reception: allow seating for at least one third of the guests, more if elderly or disabled.
- Short fork buffet reception: allow seating for half the guests.
- Buffet lunch or dinner: all need seats.

Dance floor
- 1 square metre/3 square feet per person. Example: for 150 guests you will need a dance floor space of 5.5 metres/18 square feet. Not all will be dancing at the same time.

SPECIAL DIETS

You will almost certainly have to deal with special diets for people with allergies, who are diabetic, those who are on a low cholesterol diet or who follow a low salt regime.

Generally speaking, those with medical conditions or those who follow strict eating guidelines will know what they can or can't eat. If the customer explains to a staff member that they are avoiding a particular ingredient it is important for that staff member to find out from the chef if the diner's choice avoids these items. Guessing just won't do.

Allergies

Allergies can include the gluten in wheat, rye and barley. This allergy is known as coeliac. Other allergies include peanuts and all derivatives, sesame seeds, cashews, pecans, brazil or walnuts as well as milk, fish, shellfish and eggs.

Diabetic

In those with diabetes, the body is unable to control the level of glucose within the blood. Diets include avoiding high sugar dishes and some from the low cholesterol list below.

Low cholesterol

People with high cholesterol need to avoid polyunsaturated fats and limit animal fats. Food that can be eaten includes lean meat, fish, fruit and vegetables plus low fat milk, cheese and yoghurt.

Low salt (or sodium)

People on a low salt diet sometimes have reduced salt in their food, and sometimes no salt at all.

Vegans

Vegans, like vegetarians, don't eat meat or fish. In addition, they won't eat anything of animal origin, such as milk and honey. They will eat vegetables, vegetable oils, cereals, fruits and seeds.

Cultural and religious diets

As our culture becomes more diverse, it is important to be aware of differing requirements and ways of cooking allowed by certain faiths.

Muslims:

◆ no meat, offal or animal fat unless it is halal meat (as required by Islamic dietary law).

Jews:

◆ no pork or pork products;
◆ no shellfish;
◆ no animal fats or gelatine from animals considered to be unclean or not slaughtered according to the prescribed manner;
◆ restrictions on methods of preparation and cooking practices;
◆ preparation and eating of meat and dairy produce at the same meal not allowed.

Sikhs:

◆ no beef or pork;
◆ no halal meat;
◆ may prefer a vegetarian diet.

Hindus:

◆ no beef;
◆ rarely pork;
◆ some Hindus will not eat any other meats, fish or eggs.

DRINKS

As a caterer, you will be asked to advise on wines and buy them in for certain functions. However, many smaller caterers have little involvement as their customers supply their own wines. You can charge a corkage for larger parties as your profits will be affected but I tend not to for small parties. You must feel your way in this as it will differ from client to client, party to party.

To help you with your wine service, the following pages outline wine buying, storage, serving wine, how to deal with corked bottles and the types of wine to match with food. I also look at wine diversity and there is a helpful wine vocabulary list.

Coffee, tea and water are also covered here, this trinity equally important for the caterer to get right.

WINE

Obviously, if you're running a business specialising in sandwiches, then wine is of no commercial interest. But for other types of catering, it has taken on a very distinctive role.

Choice of wine is of paramount importance. If you don't have enough knowledge to source wines to match your food, seek the advice of a wine consultant or perhaps approach a wine writer. They have a great knowledge of the trade and attend many wine tastings. Also, they are generally freelance and so not tied to a particular supplier or producer.

Wine buying and storage

A good supplier will hold tastings for you and your staff and will keep cases in storage for you, with the wines kept at the right temperature. A supplier, consultant or wine writer will go through the menu with you and marry wines to go with the food.

> **♦ TIP ♦**
>
> You will only need space for storing wine when bought for a particular event. You won't need to have wine stocks as this ties up your capital.

Tips for storing wine

♦ The older wines get, the more carefully they need to be treated.

♦ Wine doesn't like wildly fluctuating temperatures, vibration or warmth.

♦ Red wine should be stored at 14–16°C and white wine at 10–12°C.

♦ Wine should be stored on its side, never upright.

♦ Most cellars are perfect for wine storage as they keep the wines at a constant cool temperature and the corks don't dry out. But cellars aren't necessary as you will be moving the wines quickly from wine merchant to client.

> **♦ TIP ♦**
>
> Wine should be stored in dark, secure, ventilation-free area which can be locked.

A diverse wine list

Gone are the days when French wine dominated the wine list. Wines from Australia, New Zealand, South Africa, Chile, Argentina, Spain, Italy and to a lesser extent, the USA, Germany and Eastern Europe are chosen thanks to the growth of wine retailing. And, of course, there have been vast improvements in wine making, Canada's British Columbia wines a case in point. The perfect climate, increased professionalism and diverse grape-growing makes this an area to keen an eye on. Don't dismiss other countries' wines just because they may be unknown to you. The Lebanon, for example, has a long history of good wine making.

Just as our food is becoming more global, so is our wine. You can choose wines to match the diversity of the food on your menus. This might include previously unknown grapes such as the spicy, fleshy Viognier, the musky, aromatic Pinot Gris, the plummy voluptuous Merlot and the rich, spicy Shiraz.

Go beyond the Chardonnays of this world. They have dominated the market for far too long and are seen as a desperately over-oaked cliché. But there are excellent ones too, particularly from France. Just be discriminating as some of the new world ones can overwhelm the food.

Tips for choosing wine

♦ Avoid well-known supermarket wines. Customers know their price and may be appalled by the mark-up.
♦ Don't pawn the kitchen off with inferior wines to cook with. The poor quality will, regrettably, show.
♦ The cooler the climate, the leaner the wine. The alcohol percentage can be as low as 9–11 per cent.
♦ In hotter climates, wines will have tropical fruit flavours, many having a robust 14–15 per cent alcohol content.

Tips for serving wine

♦ Choose glasses that complement wine. Don't even think of serving wine, no matter how inexpensive it is, in Paris goblets.
♦ Choose instead a plain, clear glass with a generously sized bowl that tapers slightly before the rim. The stem should be long enough so the glass is held by the stem, not the bowl, as body warmth will heat up the wine.
♦ Clean glasses properly, making sure that there is no washing liquid residue on the rim as this will destroy the taste of any wine.
♦ Glasses need to be stored bowl up, not stem up, to stop trapping stale air.
♦ Chill white wines but not too much as this can dull their aroma and flavour.
♦ Red wines can be over-warmed in a warm environment so take care where you store them, e.g. not near radiators, in a hot kitchen, in the bar by the coffee machine or by bright lights.
♦ There is no need to pull the cork on wines an hour ahead of drinking. The majority of wines these days don't really need opening up as in past times when reds were likely to be tough and tannic.
♦ Waiting staff should know about the wine chosen by the client.

◆ Train staff to open a bottle properly by cutting the foil and removing the cork. Never try to extract a stubborn cork by placing the bottle between the knees and yanking it out.

◆ Train staff too to pour wine only half to two-thirds full in the glass so that guests can enjoy the aroma, leaving room to swirl the wine around the glass.

Corked and other undrinkable wine

Corked wine has a musty, dank smell caused by cork contamination. It should be replaced. White wine with a sherry smell and usually with a dark yellow colour has been oxidised (too much air via the cork). If it smells like a bad egg or a drain, then there is too much sulphur in the wine.

Thin, sharp wine may not be to everyone's taste but if it's sour then it definitely shouldn't be served. Stewed, baked, rather flabby red wine usually means over-fermentation. Nor should this be served.

◆ TIP ◆

Return all corked or tainted wine back to your suppliers.

Wine and food

Traditionally, white wine went with fish, red with meat. In Britain, with a less strong food culture and in contrast to Europe where food has changed little in comparison, we have borrowed extensively from the globe.

As a result, the guide book has been jettisoned. There are no hard and fast rules and no dire combinations that set the teeth on edge. You may argue that plainly cooked fish isn't suited to a robust tannic red, but serve it with a fruity light red and it is a successful marriage.

◆ TIP ◆

Most meals benefit from having a lighter wine first then a fuller-bodied one, a drier wine before a sweeter one, a younger wine before a vintage one. Raw, steamed and poached food is more suited to a light wine, robust wines going better with roasts and chargrills.

Dessert wines are fast growing in popularity. Chill well and serve them in small glasses. Once opened, dessert wines will keep for longer than other wines. Look beyond the ubiquitous Muscat de Beaumes de Venise. The choice is sensational. And good for profit margins.

Below is a general guide as to what type of wine suits what food but, as mentioned, the rules are there to be broken.

Whites and rosé
◆ Crisp, dry, fresh whites: salads, chicken and fish.
◆ Smooth, medium-bodied whites: pasta, creamy sauces, chicken, salmon.
◆ Full-bodied rich whites: lobster, turbot, slightly spicy style of Pacific Rim cooking.
◆ Aromatic and medium-dry whites: Riesling with spicy Thai food, Gewurtztraminer with Chinese, Tokay-Pinot Gris with foie gras.
◆ Rosé: making a comeback. Good with sharply dressed salads, summer food.

Reds
◆ Light, fruity reds: pasta, pizzas, chicken, vegetarian dishes.
◆ Smooth, medium-bodied reds: almost anything, French ones more suited to classic French dishes.
◆ Full-bodied reds: beef, game, casseroles and cold weather food. An enthusiast's wine.

Champagne and sparkling wines
They are surprisingly versatile. A richer, fuller-flavoured champagne can be drunk throughout a meal but try demi-sec champagne with fruit-based desserts as dry champagne with a rich dessert doesn't work too well.

Dessert wines
These are pure nectar. Muscats and sweet Bordeaux go well with apple, pear and peach desserts. Australian liqueur Muscats partner chocolate with dash. Mavrodaphne of Patras, a red Greek dessert wine matches chocolate too.

> ◆ TIP ◆
>
> People go first of all for the wine price, then the country of origin and then the grape.

Wine vocabulary

AOC: appellation d'origine controlée, created by French authorities to establish specific areas of production, grape varieties and which also covers maximum yield per hectare, sugar and alcohol, pruning of the vine, cultivation and wine making methods.

Alcohol: an essential element in wine, alcohol is created when enzymes created by yeasts change the sugar content of the grape juice into alcohol, carbon dioxide and heat.

Aroma: the wine's scent defined by the type of grape(s), fermentation and the age of the wine. The bouquet.

Barrel fermented: wine that is fermented in oak barrels rather than stainless steel tanks.

Blanc de Blancs: literally 'white of whites', a white wine made with white grapes like a Champagne from Chardonnay grapes.

Blanc de Noirs: white wine made from black grapes.

Blending: also known as assemblage, this is the mixing of types of wine varieties to make a more balanced wine. Bordeaux wines are usually a blend of cabernet sauvignon, cabernet franc and merlot fermented grapes.

Body: a wine with good tannic structure and good ageing potential.

Botrytis: a mould that attacks grapes either as grey rot which may endanger the harvest or as noble rot, used to make luscious dessert wines such as Sauternes and the Hungarian Tokaji.

Claret: the British name for Bordeaux red wines.

Cru: literally 'a growth', from French. It dates back to 1855 and denotes a vineyard's rank in Bordeaux which then divided into five classes or crus.

Cuvee: literally, a vatful.

Decanting: the separating of sediment of a wine. Decanting from the bottle to a glass container adds more oxygen to the wine to make it more palatable. If the wine is old, it can be a disaster as it can mean a quicker deterioration.

Fermentation, alcoholic: transformation of the sugar in the must into alcohol and carbon dioxide in the presence of yeast.

Fortified: a wine which has had added wine spirit (brandy) to it, like port or sherry.

Kabinett: high-quality German wines.

Must: unfermented grape juice obtained by crushing or pressing.

NV: non-vintage.

Oxidised wine: sherry-like or nutty flavour caused by the action of oxygen on wine due mainly to exposure to air, heat and light.

Reserve: for special cuvees (vats) set aside for ageing or for future use. It also refers to a minimum ageing period for certain spirits like Calvados, Cognac or Armagnac.

Sec, secco, seco: 'dry' in French, Italian and Portuguese or Spanish.

Spatlese: late-harvested German wines.

Tannin: different types of tannins created by the stalks, pips and skins from grapes plus nuts, wood bark and berries which are released during the fermentation process and the pressing. These tannins give the wine its specific character and contributes to its ageing. Wine storage in new wood allows extra tannins to be absorbed from the wood fibres to the wine.

Varietal: a wine made from a single grape variety. In France the wine must contain 100 per cent of the same variety but in other countries small proportions of other varieties may be added.

Vintage: originally meaning the annual grape harvest, now meaning a wine from the harvest of a particular year. Each vintage depends on a combination of climatic factors which determine the wine's quality and potential for ageing.

WATER, COFFEE AND TEA

Due to stringent drink-drive laws, we have become more of a nation of wine, water and soft drink drinkers. Gone are the days of heavy spirit drinking in favour of less alcohol at some functions so make sure you offer your clients these alternatives. However, there is a tendency to drink to excess at larger functions so do be aware of this unfortunate current trend. Discuss with your client the amount of alcohol they wish to offer.

Importantly, as a result, water, tea and coffee need to be considered as well as the alcohol.

Water

Water is almost automatically asked for by clients these days; there is a huge upsurge in demand for sparkling and still water. A remarkable two billion bottles were bought in 2003.

I tend to offer bottled water in glass bottles at events as they look smarter than plastic bottles. But don't compromise on the quality. Do check with your client which is preferred: glass, plastic, sparkling, still or flavoured water.

Coffee

It's worth experimenting with sourcing good suppliers, and if possible, go on coffee courses to understand the art of coffee. Then insist on a good grinder for those wonderful beans you have so assiduously sourced for the freshest coffee around. However, there is some superb ground coffee too.

Have the right cups and saucers to show off your coffee. Dainty or 1970s squat, canteen-like cups are not suitable. Larger, simple, straight-sided cups are best with small ones for espresso only.

◆ TIP ◆

Teas are on the increase in popularity. Do offer quality ones including peppermint and other flavoured teas.

9

Designing Menus

Your menus are the first reason people are attracted to your catering business. They showcase the kitchen's abilities and strengths, and represent the coming together of the caterer, supplier and style you offer.

It is vitally important to get your menus right, and your starting point is sourcing the ingredients. This chapter puts forward the argument that catering is all about good sourcing of any product, be it chicory, cheese, chicken, chives, chocolate or coffee. It also argues for food consistency, for the caterer to celebrate produce, good food combinations and good cooking practices.

This chapter covers:

◆ what to cook;
◆ menu balance and planning;
◆ dish creation guidelines;
◆ top tips for better cooking;
◆ keeping customers happy;
◆ quality of produce.

CREATING A MENU

In order to create a menu, these basic principles are vital: understanding produce, understanding combinations, understanding how to cook them and knowing the customer base. The following will give you some guidelines.

Food consistency

Your food has to be consistent. Of course the 'wow' factor is important but even more so is the consistency of the food that emerges from the kitchen to your client. Your customers will desert you in droves if the food on their plate doesn't match the last meal they enjoyed that you created for them. If standards are allowed to slip then you must re-examine your kitchen's strengths.

If you go down the complex food route there is more chance that it will go wrong. If you change your chef, or if you as the chef are ill, the replacement may be unable to rise to the challenge. Then you risk losing your audience if his or her skills are not as great as the previous chef.

Therefore, simplicity is the best way forward.

But even simplicity demands care and attention to detail, and knowing what goes with what. Just simply throwing a whole lot of good ingredients together without the knowledge of good food marriages will result in a horrid mishmash of tastes and ill-judged flavours.

Garnishing your food

Be wary of over-elaboration. This can be seen by some caterers as adding a touch of sophistication to their dishes. But it could add confusion and totally unnecessary clutter to the plate. What does a slice of orange have to do with a crispy duck and puy lentil salad or a salmon dish? Nothing. Don't even think of over-garnishing. More is less and never more so than on a plate. Food should look like food, not some fanciful concoction.

First-rate vs poor quality produce

If a caterer goes down the route of sourcing second-rate produce it won't taste any better if served on the finest china or the finest, whitest linen.

A good, honest caterer who passionate about the business and customers will go out of his or her way to source the best produce around. This doesn't have to mean flying in duck from Paraguay or caviar from the Caspian.

What it means is:

◆ finding carrots that have flavour and cooking them with interest and knowledge;
◆ locating a free-range chicken that really tastes like chicken and not blotting paper;
◆ tracking down very well-hung beef of note;
◆ buying good quality chocolate with high cocoa solids for the best chocolate tart;
◆ finding a herb specialist who will supply French, not flavourless Russian, tarragon;
◆ sourcing the basics with understanding and passion: bread, butter, coffee, wine.

A good caterer understands that the way to perfection is via superb produce. They know that the culinary job is simply to present these tracked-down flavours to the customer.

Don't go looking for difficulty. If certain produce is not available or is tricky to obtain on a regular basis, don't put that dish on the menu. Caterers must have peace of mind when ordering to fulfil a menu's promise.

What to cook and why to cook it

Cook what you like eating yourself and you will be halfway there. But if you have a narrow palate you may be in the wrong job! Don't cook what you don't understand. If sauces aren't up your street, but an understanding and pleasure in cooking imaginative vegetarian food is, make this your forte.

Women chefs and caterers do tend to like cooking food they understand, their raison d'etre as a chef often being to give pleasure via the table. It is a huge buzz doing just this as I and many other women chefs and caterers can testify. Many male chefs have the notion that they have to show off. Why?

◆ EXPERIENCE ◆

Alice Waters, the remarkable and much-loved Californian restaurateur of Chez Panisse who started the trend of looking for the best produce cooked simply (and if she couldn't find it she grew it) is reported to have said:

'I opened a restaurant so that people could come and eat; remember that the final goal is to nourish and nurture those who gather at your table. It is there, within this nurturing process, that I have found the greatest satisfaction and sense of accomplishment.'

I think that the same can be said of catering.

MENU PLANNING AND DISH CREATION

Planning the menu is an essential part of eating well. Professional chefs and caterers plan their menus with care, taking into account tastes, fashions, trends, health, seasonal food, limitations of time, budget and practicality.

When compiling ideas and seeking inspiration for the menu, look firstly at what you wish to achieve, who you wish to attract, what the kitchen can handle in terms of staff numbers, ability and equipment and the cost involved in each dish to produce.

Many chefs and caterers have a germ of an idea in mind when creating new dishes. Talking to people, reading about dishes in the restaurant guides, in newspapers, magazines, seeing dishes created on television by the likes of Gary Rhodes, Rick Stein, Nigella Lawson, Jamie Oliver, Delia Smith *et al* may spark off an idea.

It pays to think each idea through quite thoroughly before putting it on the menu:

◆ How much pre-prepping will this dish require?
◆ Can it be costed out favourably enough to be put on the menu?
◆ Where do the ingredients come from?
◆ Does it fit in with other dishes on the menu or does it upset the balance of fish, meat, vegetarian and sweet dishes?

Menu balance

Look at whether you now have too many cheese/fish/pork or chicken dishes. Will it look good? Think about whether there too many same-coloured dishes, too many browns and beiges, too many dishes with dairy produce or too many chilli-hot offerings. Is there a lot of fried food, or three types of the ubiquitous salmon?

What to ask yourself when working out a menu

It can take several years of cooking in a professional kitchen to reach the stage of knowing instinctively what will work and what won't work in your kitchen. But don't let the creative process be stilted by fear or indecision. Try out your ideas, present them to your team, to friends and family and ask them.

Or try them out on trusty clients (give them a sample, don't try things out on them when catering for them) who will welcome an opportunity to be of use and be flattered by being asked.

In the early days of putting a menu together when new to the business, money and time can be wasted. Questions that need answering include:

◆ Is it a worthwhile dish to develop?
◆ Are the ingredients available?
◆ What would my gross profit be on this dish?
◆ Does it present well?
◆ Can I delegate others to do this dish in my absence, or do my current kitchen staff not have the skills?

Customers, regular ones, like to see familiar dishes on the menu as well as being offered new ones. Consult them when discussing their event.

When creating tailor-made menus do look out for the number of hot and cold starters appearing on it. If you put too many hot ones on, and if you are in an unfamiliar kitchen, you will slow down the process of getting food out quickly to hungry guests. Getting that balance right is very important.

CREATE CONTENTED CUSTOMERS

Getting the temperature of the food right is crucial. Do you fiddle about trying to create a tower of jumbled ingredients, the food getting colder by the second?

Or do you simply present your food with a quick whisk of cooked food to the plate, dress it minimally and get it out to those waiting guests? Avoid having food returned because it is too cold. It will put a great deal of pressure on you when you can least afford it – in the middle of getting food out to a large number of guests, for example. If the hot dish was too time-consuming to arrange on the plate, it's time to re-think offering this one to a large party again.

Be aware too that there is nothing new under the sun when it comes to creating new dishes. It's just reinvention of the culinary wheel but with top ingredients and good cooking, your food will stand out.

Taste what you put on the menu

Good caterers and chefs always taste. One young chef I interviewed for my chefs' column arrogantly told me that he didn't need to taste the food he cooked as he had tasted it once and 'that was enough'. Stuff and nonsense.

A good chef always tastes, tastes and tastes. The reason? Your salmon terrine might have a less strong tarragon added so it needs more, you may have not put enough lemon juice or salt and freshly ground pepper in. That ice cream needs more vanilla or coffee, the prawn and coconut dish could do with some more chilli. Could the rouille for the fish soup do with extra garlic?

GOOD FOOD COMMUNICATION BETWEEN KITCHEN AND WAITING STAFF

Good caterers and chefs always discuss the menu with waiting staff so that they can talk to guests with knowledge. If staff just shrug their shoulders or say 'I'll just ask the chef what's in this dish,' it will create a bad impression to say the least. There must be harmony and communication between cook and server.

What is your style? Do you have one? Does creativity and ambition show in the cooking? If you do have style, do it with conviction. Do things your way and don't copy.

The Automobile Association Guide's ten top tips for better restaurant cooking

(Also applicable to caterers)

1. Source your suppliers carefully. Demand the best and only serve the best.

2. Use local produce where possible – if it's good enough.

3. Have one eye on the seasons – although most foods are available all year round, they nevertheless tend to be at their best for only one season.

4. Cook real food from whole raw ingredients.

5. Keep it simple, be true to the ingredients. Don't be creative just for the sake of it.

6. Always question – how can I improve this dish?

7. Taste the food you create. And remember the diner is eating more than just a forkful – so as a plateful, will it be too much, too heavy, too rich, or just plain boring?

8. Keep a sense of balance. Don't overcook, don't undercook, don't over-sauce, don't under-sauce, don't under-season. This sounds really basic, but it's where many meals fail.

9. Eat out. Get to know what the competition's doing. [For caterers: eat out and develop your skills and knowledge]

10. Don't cook for accolades. The best food comes from a kitchen that has confidence in its own ability, where the chef is in tune with the needs of the restaurant's [catering company's] customer base.

MENU WRITING

As a restaurant critic my heart can sometimes sink when reading a menu and I think, 'There is nothing that inspires me here.' Why is this? Could it be that the menu is written in flowery language – 'puddles of chive essence,' 'a mosaic of...' 'a symphony of...' with multitudes of coulis? And what, for heaven's sake, is a 'chef's special'? Something that the kitchen has too much of and is desperate to shift?

It could also be that the balance is decidedly off-putting or the menu itself is poorly presented. Is it difficult to decipher the-over-the-top handwriting? I, and many others who take a great interest in menus and their readability, find the Harvesters of this world and other fast food, so called 'family' restaurants, confusing and very, very long. But by analysing the menu you find that most of the ingredients turn up time and time again under a different guise. Rather like Chinese menus.

For caterers, most of the above applies. Make sure your menu inspires, is well balanced and that you don't duplicate ingredients. Sun-dried tomatoes in four of the five first courses you suggest, for example, is not a good idea.

◆ TIP ◆

When writing your menu, tone down the descriptions, and don't add all the ingredients, as it will only confuse.

10

Food Suppliers

Your food will be judged on its quality; you must choose your suppliers with utmost care.

This chapter covers:

◆ quality of produce;
◆ finding good local or national suppliers;
◆ sourcing alternatives in Britain and abroad;
◆ the Slow Food Movement;
◆ a useful contact list.

FINDING SUPPLIERS

Taste. Taste. Taste. If you have a good chutney at a restaurant, some excellent cheese, a smoked duck to die for, ask how to find these suppliers. Talk to restaurateurs, the generous-hearted ones only too willing to pass on good suppliers to you. And the ones to avoid.

Get price lists. Ask for samples. Bargain. Ask for wholesale prices. Consider buying by mail order. Go to as many exhibitions as possible to find the best quality food around.

I keep an eye out in delicatessens and take down the company's name of products I wish to sample. Consult the *Yellow Pages* for other sources, go on the web to locate cheese companies and other specialist companies. Cross the channel to buy more cheaply if you're in the south of England and you can spare the time. But always think quality. Always ask to taste anything before buying. It's quite normal in France!

If you can, visit Borough Market, Borough Street, London, SE1 near London Bridge (0207 407 1002) for a short cut to finding superb produce.

Contact New Covent Garden Market in London (info@cgma.gov.uk) and other major fruit and vegetable markets in your area for suppliers.

Once you have narrowed down your suppliers and start buying from them, always check your supplies, throw anything back at them that doesn't have quality stamped all over it (in the nicest possible way of course) and establish an excellent working rapport with them. This way they will look after you and will bend over backwards to keep your business. Always promptly query any accounting error and pay your bills on time.

◆ TIP ◆

You are not joined at the hip with your suppliers. Continue to locate even better ones.

Suppliers will usually call you to find out what your order is if you run a busy business. Or call them. There is usually an after-hours ordering service to leave messages for next day delivery.

TIPS FOR BUYING

◆ **Fish** is selling fast these days. Always but always have the freshest fish. Once it's past its best, toss it. Or be prepared to lose a customer.

◆ **Game** is gaining momentum thanks to its healthy eating tag. There is wild and farmed game and do try venison and boar on your menu. Wonderful.

◆ **Beef:** demand longer hanging for your beef from your supplier. 28 days or over, nothing less. Look out for darker coloured, marbled meat.

◆ **Vegetables:** insist on the best for intense flavour. Go organic for tastier vegetables. Try different varieties. There's more to life than carrots.

◆ **Fruit:** it is worth doing some research to find really tasty fruit, apples in particular. Woolly peaches, dull apples and strawberries abound.

◆ **Cheese:** find a good supplier, or three. Shop around for regional ones. Make sure your waiting staff can identify the cheeses when serving them.

◆ **Smoked salmon:** there is some truly awful smoked salmon out there. Be discerning.

◆ **Chocolate:** don't just buy any chocolate. Source one with high cocoa solids.

◆ **Coffee** finishes off a good meal with character. Make sure yours is memorable. Source the best and you'll gain extra brownie points from clients.

SOURCING YOUR INGREDIENTS

When I started as chef/restaurateur of Soanes, Petworth, West Sussex, in the 1980s, local produce was unobtainable. Excellent fish, vegetables and cheeses had to come from Covent Garden or Rungis, the Paris market.

Only the local butcher and a mushroom forager offered goods I was seeking. I grew herbs and some vegetables and salads. Local wholesale suppliers could only offer second-class vegetables and fruit, dull, tasteless salads, even poorer tomatoes. The couldn't care less attitude was deeply dispiriting, hence the long-distance sourcing.

The signs are promising. There is a stealthy trend for caterers and restaurateurs, the better ones, to offer locally – or regionally – sourced sausages, cheeses, meat, vegetables, fruit and drink to their customers. They prefer to know the provenance of their supplies. But does the quality shine, is the produce chosen with knowledge? Or is the buying of local and regional food merely paying lip service to trends?

Does the client really know or mind? Or, worse still, are they unable to tell the difference between a carrot grown with care around the corner to a mass-produced Dutch or British hothouse one? Our tastebuds, having been assaulted by over-processed food for years, could be immune to quality now that large servings of cheap food are the consumer yardstick.

There does, however, seem to be a growing band of people with heightened expectations, resulting in the raising of standards by local and regional producers. They relish the difference and vote with their feet, choosing catering companies, restaurants and pubs that source the best around without the stabilisers, additives and other 'benefits' of mass-produced food.

◆ TIP ◆

Today's restaurateurs and caterers are spoilt for choice if they wish to source quality ingredients which are local, regional and seasonal. The added advantage is that it helps to cut food miles and, as a result, pollution and fuel consumption.

Sourcing alternatives

The alternatives for local food sourcing are supermarkets, local wholesale and retail, cash and carry, specialist food companies and farmers' markets.

The choice is vast, the quality variable. Caterers often source their produce from a mix of the above, but remember to price items diligently. Cash and carry companies aren't necessarily cheaper. Carry a notepad with your basics listed and do spot checks on prices.

There's no sense either in buying in bulk from cash and carry if you are unable to use the product before its sell-by date or if you have limited storage space. Impulse buying rarely pays off and just creates problems rather than solving them.

Use specialist companies sparingly as their goods tend to be for the well-heeled personal shopper and not for the caterer interested in profit. Ask for discounts as a caterer. They will offer you a percentage off the price but the cost of transport will remove this small advantage so you really have to weigh up the advantages of buying from this source.

If buying from a specialist company, do make sure you order a good amount of any produce you are sure to use (jars, tins and vacuum-packs keep well) to save on the transport costs. But only if you will use them. You don't want to spend money on them only for them to gather dust and take up valuable space. It's a false economy.

How not to source your food

There are many national wholesale suppliers like Brakes (formerly Brake Bros) whose lorries criss-cross Britain and France, their buying power and market dominance creating an astonishing £1.4 billion annual turnover.

There is no need for caterers or chefs to do any cooking whatsoever if sourcing Brake products. Cocktail BBQ Chicken drumlettes, Brake Crinkle Cut fries and Peach and Champagne Tart were all medal winners at the 2003 British Frozen Food Federation Annual Awards.

The major supplier of frozen, chilled and ambient foods to the trade including J.D. Wetherspoons across the UK, Brakes' corporate message is a chilling one. 'Consumer and market trends,' 'product assessment,' 'total solution provider,' 'customer to really focus on ... developing their branded estate,' 'cost controls,' 'pouch, c-pet tray or multi-portion foil' packaging with nary a foray into selling food with passion or indeed a regional or local slant.

Readymade soups, boeuf bourguionne (sic), mashed potato or salmon mousse to free up the 'busy chef' for executive paperwork – Brakes' recipes are all part of the service.

Witness Baked Garlic Chicken and Pancake Tagliatelle, cited product numbers given: 'Simply thaw one Chicken Supreme (3042) and smother in garlic and herb cream cheese. Wrap in two rashers of thawed Beechwood Smoked Back Bacon (2806) and pan fry in 5 g butter for seven minutes each side.' Then you're asked to toss in Chopped Garlic (4017), shredded French Butter Crepes (3160) and Mange Tout (4741) in some more butter. Sprinkle with Finely Chopped Parsley (4019).

Voilà! You are a chef! No need to get down and dirty by doing the leg work in good food sourcing or real cooking, let alone think.

3663 (spells 'food' on your keyboard) is another nationwide wholesale company whose sales are also over £1 billion a year. It offers frozen and chilled food delivered by 1,000 vehicles to over 50,000 customers in the catering trade, including Pret à Manger. Their 600-strong Smart Choice range includes ready meals, sauces, soups, canned produce and ice creams. Sales are booming. Think of those food miles by both companies. Think of the quality.

Food for thought

The less we know of food via family, home economics, school meals and eating meals in a social setting, and where food comes from, how it is grown, reared and produced, the less good, well-sourced food will matter.

If this is the public mindset of the future, hard-working, caring, responsible caterers and chefs may be fighting a losing battle to move sourcing to an altogether higher level of quality. Good produce and skilful cooking may mean little to the next generation of caterers, chefs – and customers.

◆ **TIP** ◆

Raymond Blanc, chef/owner of the Manoir Aux Quat' Saisons in Oxfordshire says that 'British chefs desperately need to sharpen up. They're not connected with their food.'

He adds: 'How can we encourage the UK to move from cheap food to "real food"? This applies to everyone's food, not just in the restaurant trade.' It of course applies to the catering trade too.

The British Protected Food Names Scheme

The EU Protected Food Names Scheme (PFNS), a British version of the *appellation controlée* system that exists in France to safeguard their wines, has been in operation for 11 years with Cornish clotted cream and Jersey Royal potatoes as prime examples. PFNS' raison d'etre is to protect regional and traditional foods whose authenticity and origin can be guaranteed through independent inspection. But who is aware of PFNS? Not many. Seek out this scheme to find out more.

Sourcing food from Britain and abroad

There is no doubt that eating is even more pleasurable when you know where the food on your plate comes from, be it regional or local. Or, indeed, whether the olive oil or balsamic vinegar has been derived with passion and erudition from abroad.

Obviously not all produce can come from this country. The best foie gras, black pudding, cured hams like Parma, specialist cheeses, pistachios, limes, lentils and most wines are just a trickle of global riches to our shores. You really don't have to go any further to find such riches in our midst than supermarkets, wholesalers and delicatessens.

The Slow Food Movement

Carlo Petrini is president of Slow Food, the 18-year-old association that was formed to defend Italian regional foods and is now an international movement with 80,000 members. He declares that 'a gastronome who isn't an environmentalist is a fool,' adding that people must know where food comes from and how it's produced.

The association protects traditional foods at risk of extinction in many countries and safeguards breeds of animals, wines, pulses, vegetables, fruits, cheeses, cured meat and fish. To find out more go to their website: www.slowfood.com.

QUALITY AND PROVENANCE OF PRODUCE

Do we care enough as consumers? We have a vested interest in helping beleaguered farmers who look for alternatives in keeping their farms afloat, their animals' welfare and the quality of all yields at the top of the agenda. But only if they can come up with the goods, not for nostalgia or purely for loyalty. The produce has to stand out.

The same applies to all produce in this new marketplace of small suppliers where taste and quality must be the foremost criteria. Since 1979, UK growers' produce has dwindled to supplying just four per cent of fruit and 52 per cent of the vegetables we eat. Mange tout from Peru travels 6,312 miles, green beans from southern Africa 5,979 miles.

Polytunnels

These large polythene tunnels, used as greenhouses, now produce up to 80 per cent of summer fruit. Five thousand acres alone of Herefordshire, Kent and Scotland alone are now pastures of plastic. The season has been extended by months thanks to this method of growing. Just down the road from me is Tangmere airfield, part of the Battle of Britain strategy and now one of Europe's largest pepper nurseries with over 50 acres of glasshouses on its 115 acres of land.

Salads, herbs, vegetables, flowers and ingredients, previously more likely to have been flown in from other parts of the world, are now grown in polytunnels. The defence from growers is that it is British, good for local economy and something we should be proud of, despite the desecration of the landscape.

Growth of polytunnels

The growth of polytunnels is largely due to supermarkets which demand reliable, unblemished fruit and vegetables. Ethnic restaurant chefs benefit from being able to source some of their produce such a pak choy. However, the quality and variety is not good according to Nahm, the London Thai restaurant, which has to import its fernleaf, tumeric, lemongrass and other ingredients directly from Bangkok. K. Martin & Son, small Lincolnshire producers, supply Indian restaurants with specialist herbs including methi (fenugreek) from their polytunnels.

The Guardian newspaper gardener, Monty Don, mounted a campaign with others against strawberries, 'tasteless junk fruit' grown in 250 acres of 'ugly polytunnels' near his Herefordshire home when the company S. & A. Davies began building an 18-acre labour camp of 300 mobile homes and amenity centre. And he won. He, I and countless others query the quality of produce grown in these polytunnels, the scarring of the landscape, and the exploitation in some cases of migrant workers.

Caterers play a big part alongside restaurateurs and the public in demanding food that tastes of something. The current British strawberry is 'helped' along by 17 fungicides and 16 insecticides and still tastes of nothing.

In the 20 years since I started catering there has been much to celebrate. As caterers, customers, chefs and restaurateurs, we need to keep the pressure on for a greener, more sustainable, definitely tastier Britain.

USEFUL CONTACTS FOR SOURCING PRODUCE

Government agencies are included in this list. There are plenty of other producers to discover. Consult the *Yellow Pages*, your local council and websites via Google or other search engines. Also look at the chef suppliers' directory (Hotelkeeper & Caterer): 0208 62 4700 or email chotsen@rbi.co.uk.

> ◆ TIP ◆
>
> Just one word of warning: just because it's local doesn't necessarily mean it's good. Be choosy! Locate the best produce possible and help raise standards.

National and government agencies

National Association of Farmers' Markets: www.farmersmarkets.net

DEFRA (Department of Environment, Food and Rural Affairs):
0207 238 6687

Department of Agriculture and Rural Development (Northern Ireland):
www.dardni.gov.uk

Regional

Buckinghamshire Food Group: 01296 383345 or email: env-edt@ bucksscc.gov.uk

East Anglian Fine Foods: www.foodanddrinkforum.co.uk

East Midlands Fine Foods: www.eastmidlandsfinefood.co.uk

Food From Britain: www.foodfrombritain.com

Guild of Fine Food Retailers: wwwfinefoodworld.co.uk

Hampshire Fare: www.hampshirefare.co.uk

Heart of England Fine Foods: www.heff.co.uk

Henrietta Green's Food Lovers' Club: www.foodloversbritain.com

Highland & Islands Enterprise: www.scottishfoodanddrink.com

Kentish Fare: www.kentishfare.co.uk

Local producers: www.buylocalfood.co.uk

London Food Link: www.londonfoodlink.org

North West Fine Foods: www.nw-fine-foods.co.uk

Northumbria Larder: www.northumbria-larder.co.uk

Oxfordshire Food Group: 01865 484116 or email: localfood@brookes.ac.uk

South East Food Group Partnership: www.buylocalfood.co.uk

A Taste of Sussex at Sussex Enterprise: www.sussexenterprise.co.uk

Taste of the West: www.tasteofthewest.co.uk

Scottish Enterprise: www.scottishfoodanddrink.com

Scottish Food and Drink: 0141 228 2409

Scottish Organic Producers Association: www.sopa.org.uk

A Taste of Ulster: 0289 0665630

Tastes of Anglia: www.tastesofanglia.com

Wales: The True Taste: www.walesthetruetaste.com or 08457 775577

Welsh Development Agency: www.foodwales.co.uk

Welsh Organic meat: www.cambrianorganics.com

Yorkshire Regional Food Group: www.yorkshireregionalfoodgroup.co.uk

Specialists

British Cheese Board: www.britishcheese.com

The British Herb Association: 0207 331 7415

British Sheep Dairying Association: BSDA@btopenworld.com

The Chocolate Society: www.chocolate.co.uk

Culinary Events Ltd: events@thecheeseweb.com

Fairtrade Foundation: www.fairtrade.org.uk

The Garlic Information Centre: 01424 892440

Specialist Cheesemakers Association: www.specialistcheesemakers.co.uk

Ethnic food companies and associations

There are many more to choose from locally and nationally. Many supply via mail order.

Chinese and Asian Foods: Wing Yip: 0208 450 0422

Japanese: Yaohan Oriental Shopping Centre: 0208 200 0009

Indian ingredients: Patel Brothers: 0208 672 2792

Italian ingredients: I. Camisa and Son: 0207 437 7610

Mexican ingredients: The Cool Chile Company: 0870 902 1145

Moroccan ingredients: Le Maroc: 0208 968 9783

Spanish ingredients: R. Garcia and Sons: 0207 221 6119

11

Specialist Suppliers

This chapter deals with developing relationships with other specialist suppliers – such as florists and marquee and hire equipment companies.

You may be asked to cater for large events either by a business or a private party giver and be asked to give quotes for the following:

◆ florists;
◆ marquee hire companies;
◆ equipment hire companies;
◆ photographers;
◆ cake makers;
◆ firework specialists;
◆ toastmasters;

- wine companies;
- staff hire agencies;
- children's entertainers;
- musicians;
- projectionists;
- dancers;
- speakers;
- magicians.

Keep a list of those you meet along the way in your catering business, or who you like the look of, such as your local florist. Or contact a number of those on the list to find out what they offer and their price. If you cater for a party and the host provides terrific musicians or other talent, ask for details so that you can add them to your growing list. They will be only too happy to be recommended by you to clients. Find out what they charge and if they add any extras on such as travel expenses.

DEALING WITH SPECIALISTS

There are two ways of dealing with specialists: getting them to quote directly with the client or taking on the work yourself and adding a percentage to the final bill. The latter requires more work on your behalf and more responsibility.

Remember to check the details each time you book someone. For example, if you are dealing with musicians directly and taking a percentage, make sure that they haven't changed their per hour rate and that they haven't decided to give up classical music in favour of rhythm and blues. You might have an irate client on your hands.

Also find out:

- what set up they need for electricity (they will bring and sort out their own sound system but check with them beforehand);
- any seating and meal requirements they have;
- their musical plan of action (sets to be played and for how long).

◆ TIP ◆

With any entertainment, ask how much it will cost to extend the entertainment beyond the specified time.

MARQUEE HIRE COMPANIES

When dealing with marquee hire companies who have been hired by the party giver, make sure the catering area is taken into discussion at the early planning stages. It is up to you to discuss your needs with the client first of all so that the information can be passed on to the marquee company. Preferably, have direct contact with the marquee company so that you can stipulate certain necessities. You will need to know the set up so that you can plan your party well so that client and guests are satisfied.

Some clients like to save money by squeezing inappropriately large numbers of guests into small marquees. Or, they arrange to hire a marquee that is too large for the number of guests, making the guests feel that they are in a barn. Guide them.

Working with the marquee company

When doing an outside catering job, make sure that you can liaise directly with the marquee company your clients have chosen from the beginning. A marquee is a lovely setting for an event, but it can be a bit tricky at times for the organisers. The following tips should help the events run more smoothly.

Kitchen prepping

To work effectively, you need a kitchen prepping marquee attached to the main marquee with sufficient tables, a clearing area, storage and its own entrance/exit to vehicles as well as to the main marquee.

You will need water. Make sure that you have access to a stand pipe or the premises' kitchen. If it's the kitchen, you need a way to transport water as it may be quite a distance from the marquee.

Access to the marquee

Talk to the marquee company and the client about access to the marquee. You don't want your staff to have to walk over flowerbeds or negotiate bushes in order to set up or clear – it is awkward and damage to the garden will create a rift between you and your client after the event.

Making space

Check the space between the tables and chairs. Waiting staff need to be able to serve at these tables without having to bend themselves into awkward shapes or ask guests to move their chairs so that they can get past them.

Make sure there is plenty of space for the buffet tables and bar. Guests need to have room to stand around both areas and not get in the way of seated guests. It's like being on an aeroplane and queuing for the loo: if you're the table near the buffet or bar you don't want to have people hovering around you looking anxious.

If there is a dance floor, discuss with the client and marquee suppliers where it should go so that it doesn't affect the smooth running of the catering. If your staff have to negotiate dancing couples and an ear-splitting band while clearing tables and glasses it will create problems, and your operation will look messy and unprofessional.

Getting power

Make sure you have the right requirements for power if you are plugging in fridges and cookers. You don't want to overload the system but clients are apt to ignore this fact and assume it will be all right on the night. If there are too many pieces of equipment, the system can blow.

If the marquee company is asked to provide heating by generators, make doubly and trebly sure that the client operates them. (Alternatively, find out what is necessary to run the generators yourself if they do stop working.)

Clearing up

When clearing the marquee either on the night of the party or the following morning, check for any damage to the grounds and remove all rubbish so that you won't have any awkward discussions with the client when settling the account. Liaise with the client before leaving the premises to check that everything is done and that they are happy.

Toilets

The position of the toilets is critical. Liaise with the client, the marquee company and the toilet hirers about the best place to put them. The client won't want them near the entrance as this is where their guests will enter and you don't want them too near the food preparation area. They should be easy for guests to find, even in the dark.

Security

If you want to set up your temporary kitchen in the marquee a day ahead of the party, make sure that there is adequate security. You don't want your pots and pans, wine and other goods to disappear. If this proves a problem, don't take chances and hope for the best. Set up closer to the party and have peace of mind, not a sleepless night.

Lighting

This often forgotten necessity should be discussed with the client if you are involved in an outside catering job. They may have not thought of it as they don't give this kind of large party very often – if at all – but their guests will be unable to find their cars or the hired bus to whisk them back home after the event in the late hours.

♦ TIP ♦

Remind the client about lighting for paths. If going for candles and other naked flame lighting, make sure that they are placed safely and don't create a fire hazard. Alternatively, hire lighting.

Checklist

Ask the marquee company if there is:

- **electricity** and running water.
- **a service tent.** Is it big enough to fit all the equipment in and to set up tables for preparing the food? (Boxed equipment with all the cutlery, plates and glasses take up a big space so ask for this to be taken into consideration.)
- **enough space for buffet tables and bar,** and enough space for guests to negotiate buffet tables and other tables and chairs.
- **enough space for staff** to negotiate the marquee to serve at tables and to clear.
- **enough space for the band** to play in and for the staff to get around them. Are there chairs for the band? Electrical points?
- **a separate entrance for kitchen staff** to access the catering and equipment vans.
- **enough space at the tables** – are they big enough for the numbers of people and the equipment that needs to be set up on them?
- **a rubbish** and clearing area.
- **a toilet** close to the marquee.
- **outdoor lighting** around the marquee, and to cars and toilets if the party is to finish after sunset.
- **heating** if the party is taking place other than in the high heat of summer. And are there instructions for the generators so that they don't stop working?
- **an arrangement for clearing up** the following day.

EQUIPMENT HIRE

As a one-man band, I tend to pass on the charge of hiring equipment directly to the client instead of taking a percentage as it lessens paperwork and payment. Do make sure, however, that the client is aware of all the charges including VAT and delivery costs. If you don't make this clear, the client might rightly ask you to pay for it as you didn't point it out at the beginning. If the order changes (an increase in guest numbers, the menu changes), inform your client so that they are aware of how much they are spending.

When calculating how many glasses, plates, cutlery, serving dishes, table-cloths and all the other items needed for the party, take into consideration, for example, glasses for water, wine, pre- and post-dinner drinks, glasses for staff, musicians and others who may be at the party such as drivers.

There is rarely enough time to count all the items when setting up a party but, at the end of the party when clearing away and stacking everything into their boxes, your staff can do a count. Note the losses and breakages and inform your clients so that they don't get a surprise when the invoice is sent to them with a breakage sum added to it. If you do have the time to check every item and find that some are broken, chipped, cracked or just missing, inform the hire company as soon as possible after the party.

Your staff and hired equipment

Do make sure that your staff – they may be untrained – know how to clear away efficiently and well so that these breakages and losses are kept to a minimum. For example, are they in such a hurry to get away that they throw the cutlery away with uneaten food? Or do they clear glasses badly so that they break? It is up to you to ensure that your staff are behaving responsibly and know what to do and how to do it.

♦ TIP ♦

Any unbidden, extra costs to the client are a reflection on your business so keep your clients informed and your staff in check.

TIPS FOR DEALING WITH SPECIALIST SUPPLIERS

- ♦ Set out details of the arrangements in writing with them.
- ♦ Supply them with a map, times and address for the event.
- ♦ Phone them up prior to the party to make sure that all arrangements are in place.
- ♦ Arrange for payment details.
- ♦ Get their mobile numbers and give them yours.
- ♦ Check on their whereabouts on the day. Are they lost? Do they need extra directions?

12

Staffing for Your Catering Business

Staff, as most caterers and restaurateurs will testify, are both the biggest problem and the biggest asset a business can have.

No matter how good your catering business is, it cannot survive without good staff. Your staff will enhance and reflect the qualities your business offers to clients. Nothing will do more damage to your reputation than having unhelpful, slovenly, couldn't-care-less, rude staff – apart from bad food, that is! Your clients will expect – rightly – consistent, welcoming, professional, calm, knowledgeable staff at their function.

Choose your staff with care. Surly, lazy attitudes rub off on other staff. Intimidating verbal behaviour and especially physical abuse are not to be tolerated. These traits rightly belong to the past.

562,700 jobs were taken by catering staff in 2004, employment in Britain topping 25 million. Nearly 142,000 full-time catering jobs were filled by men, over 93,000 by women. This was reversed by part timers (117,700 by men, 209,800 by women).

This chapter deals with:

◆ staffing for solo caterers and growing catering businesses;
◆ staffing problems;
◆ college and agency recruitment, casual and agency staff;
◆ catering management;
◆ job descriptions and analysis, and interviewing;
◆ explanation of kitchen hierarchy;
◆ staff organisation and training;
◆ job details, including cleaning rotas, dress code, meals, holidays, smoking, overtime, behaviour;
◆ pay legalities;
◆ basic waiting skills and management skills;
◆ communicating effectively with guests and clients.

THE IMPORTANCE OF SERVICE

Service, service, service is of paramount importance to the catering industry. As standards rise in quality produce, so must the service which, of course, covers all kitchen, waiting and cleaning staff and any other employees in a catering business.

◆ TIP ◆

Personal service and attention to detail set the best catering companies apart from their competitors.

We have entered a period of high demand of good staffing due to the booming hospitality industry but this labour supply needs to come from somewhere. Will potential employees be trained sufficiently to offer good service and high standards? This is of concern for all those engaged in the industry.

There is no doubt that the work is demanding and can be seen – still – as a dead end job by some. But, thankfully, others see it as a stimulating and rewarding challenge.

The hospitality industry is sometimes seen as theatre: catering staff forming a bond with customers (cast members), the venue itself the stage and the work as lines to be learnt. Some exponents of this profession love to entertain, but they must always remember their serious professional stance coupled with humour, good judgement and sensitivity.

Staff need direction, motivation and an incentive to carry out their work and to understand the need to be very flexible. This comes from management. All staff need to be accepted by both sexes, have the ability to make customers feel at ease and to be respected by employers.

WAITING AND KITCHEN STAFF

Waiters and waitresses – skilled ones – offer service. They are not servants. They have talked to the caterer about the composition of the food. They are aware when and how to clear a table and when not to. When to pour wine. How to work with the client.

Kitchen staff are creative in different ways. Chefs have the ability to prepare food, timing cooking to a split second with speed and accuracy. They can cook and present all dishes coming out of the kitchen with skill. And they must be able to do it time and time again to the same high standard. Consistency is all.

FINDING STAFF

Even if you are a one-man band, you will still need to find good waiting staff for your functions. You may have friends and family who wish to earn some pocket money or you may prefer to find professional staff. For a larger catering company, it will be necessary to find kitchen and waiting staff.

Catering colleges

These are one source of kitchen and waiting staff, but the standard in some is decidedly questionable. The teaching focuses on hotel-like service which is past its sell-by date, according to employers.

Flour-based sauces, soups and stocks made from packets and heavy, stodgy food are out of kilter to today's food styles. Silver service, although not favoured by restaurants these days, is useful for banqueting and is to the caterer's advantage. Folding napkins into unnecessary shapes is a waste of their – and your – time in my view. But some clients like it so you may have to find out how to do origami napkin folding if you or your staff don't possess the skills.

Some colleges have moved on thankfully, and are teaching their students the art of lighter cooking combined with slow food cooking (daubes, terrines, bread-making for example). They are sourcing their materials with care and attention, and teaching students how to run a kitchen, amongst other modern and commercial necessities. These are the chefs and waiting staff that will be able to deliver the consistently high standards that customers expect and good catering companies wish to achieve.

Staff's attitude to food

Catering companies can also be handicapped by some students' and non-trained staff's backgrounds. The type of food they experience at home can be quite at variance with food offered by the catering company which they have no interest in or desire to find out about. There can be a mountain to climb in food education, but when a staff member sees the light and becomes excited about the type and quality of the food and service it's a eureka moment.

This is a bleak outlook, I am aware. Staffing is a growing problem due to the fast food nation of eaters who know or care little about cooking or who come from a background of not eating as a family around a table. Some entering the profession see the catering trade as a way to becoming famous – and fast – to follow in the shoes of the Jamie Olivers of this world without having to work too hard. Unlike Jamie, who started from the bottom of the heap and proved himself.

Recruitment agencies

Placing a well-worded ad in local papers will hopefully attract the right kind of people. For more permanent staff such as a chef, or temporary staff such as waiting staff for functions, you may have to recruit staff through agencies.

Catering agencies are employment agencies but dedicated to this specific industry. They may place staff permanently or temporarily. There may be 30,000 vacancies on any one day in London alone due to the burgeoning catering, restaurant and hotel market. Job vacancies include head chefs, trainees, commis and sous chefs, kitchen porters, waiters and waitresses, bar staff and managers.

♦ TIP ♦

An agency charges at least 10 per cent of the agreed wage, the chef or other member of staff via the agency working a probationary period. On completion, the agency will invoice the company for their percentage.

It is important to weigh up the costs and advantages if you are recruiting agency staff. On the plus side, many agencies get to know their applicants well and match appropriate chefs and other staff to appropriate businesses. It's not in their interests to get this wrong but, of course, it can and does happen, as some agencies see the staff as merely making money for them. Agencies aren't cheap and you may achieve just as good if not better results with an ad which may attract greater numbers of applicants. Temporary staff have little or no loyalty towards your business and it may show.

Temporary agency staff usually are better paid per hour. This may cause friction once this is known by your other staff if their hourly rate doesn't match the temp's pay so try not to enter this mix if humanly possible.

If you have a larger catering company with staff, promote from within. It is easier and more cost effective to find a commis chef from an agency than to go to an agency to recruit a higher up position. Your current chef may be able to train up a commis chef to the higher grade once they have been with the company for a while.

Agencies can charge quite a hefty per hour charge, and the staff are a mixed bag of good, poor and downright dreadful. It just depends on which staff the agency can find to fill their books, so ask pertinent questions:

- What is your charge per hour?
- Does this include VAT?
- Is there an extra charge for Sunday work?
- Is there a transport charge?
- How much experience do your staff have?
- Are they trained or just casual labour?
- How many hours can they work?
- What do they expect for breaks? To eat?
- Can I have only non-smoking staff?
- How much importance does the company attach to grooming?
- What do staff wear? (You can stipulate your demands here.)
- Do they speak English? (Or whatever language you prefer.)
- Can I have all the details in writing?

◆ TIP ◆

Put your foot down with smoking breaks. Staff can smoke in their own time and it is unfair on the non-smokers who will have more work as a result. It is also unpleasant for clients and their guests to smell smoke on a member of staff's hands, clothes or breath, and it can ruin food and wine. Unfortunately, there are many smokers in the catering trade.

Other sources of recruitment
- Advertising
- Job centres
- Headhunters
- Existing staff
- Waiting list – people contacting your business looking for a job
- Previous applicants
- Casual callers
- Education systems

MOTIVATING YOUR STAFF

Is catering management unique? Every industry thinks it is unique and in a sense, each is right. A look at the industry with its uniforms, differing job titles, tipping, unsocial hours, labour mobility, irregular work flow and the degrees of entrepreneurship needed in this business, amply demonstrates that the catering industry is certainly a special case.

Due to this 'special case' scenario, one thing is for sure: you must be organised. And that means good staffing at all levels, staff who are flexible, understand speed when busy but do not forego quality. They must have the ability to do other jobs such as cleaning and undergo extra training if necessary during less busy times. Motivation by management is paramount to keeping good staff. Job satisfaction can not be underestimated.

Unskilled staff

What motivates those without skills? The reasons why unskilled catering work is popular are:

◆ the work is easy to learn;
◆ there is variety;
◆ it is not a factory;
◆ you meet people;
◆ it is convenient to have quick money and doesn't have to be permanent.

How to motivate people

It is necessary to introduce good management practices with staff in order to keep them. It is done by:

◆ clear communication. It is not possible to respond positively when there is no clarity;
◆ not over-controlling;
◆ recognising achievement. This will result in increased good performance;
◆ good teaching;
◆ rewarding adequately;
◆ reviewing performance on a regular basis;

- treating staff like human beings and not like cogs in a machine;
- avoiding making promises and favours and not delivering them;
- taking what people say seriously – listening to staff;
- investigating complaints or grievances;
- avoiding deals;
- making your staff realise they are a real team;
- recognising a career commitment.

Many people enjoy working in a team. Find things that your staff have in common, other than working for the same business, e.g. they are all students, all women, all the same age. Work on these shared characteristics and build up their bond.

Commitment to the job can also be achieved by staff being prepared to ditch old skills and learn new ones. They are empowered, and recognise their assets. Loyalty and flexibility may well be the outcome.

THE STAFF INTERVIEW

The relationship between employer and employee may start when the manager says 'Start Monday' and the applicant says 'OK'. But let's look more closely at the agreement that has been made.

Getting off to a good start

At the interview stage, the interviewer is keen to assess the capabilities of the interviewee in relation to effort, general willingness and track record (if not taking on a novice in the business). At that 'Start Monday' stage, the agreement is very imprecise and open to misinterpretation.

The employer is taking on an unspecified potential, the employee an indeterminate amount of work. Good interviewing practice, previous experience of the same type of work, references and a job description all create a more precise and mutual understanding.

A job description covers the work entailed, hours of work, shift times, payment, staff meals, behaviour and dress. But it can't describe what effort will be required. So it is a good idea to take on a willing applicant for a trial period before offering a permanent job.

If you are running a larger catering business and hiring chefs, ask them to cook a dish or two from your menu then sit down with them and, over the tasting, discuss with them the outcome and what they would be able to contribute to the menu and style of cooking.

Although this may seem like a lengthy process, at least you will be able to choose a good chef rather than one who may look good on paper but can't cook the simplest of dishes. And it will save you time and money in the long run.

During this process, you will be able to find out if the chef is familiar with and knows how to cook the ingredients on your menus. If the chef is unable to rise to the challenge of cooking the best lemon tart, or roasting fillet of beef to enhance its flavours, then you may not be talking the same culinary language.

To save time and money when looking for staff, find out as much as possible over the phone or by other means of communication before agreeing to an interview – and the cook-off.

Culinary checklist

You may also wish to have a culinary checklist to ask prospective staff about. Some possible subjects for the checklist:

What can you cook?

♦ patés and terrines;
♦ soups;

◆ breads;
◆ canapés;
◆ ice creams;
◆ sauces;
◆ dressings;
◆ game;
◆ fish;
◆ egg dishes: e.g. omelettes, Eggs Benedict.

What can you do?

◆ butchery;
◆ larder;
◆ working out GP (the kitchen's gross profits);
◆ menu costing;
◆ purchasing.

Don't underestimate the applicant who applies for a job without qualifications and experience. If the person displays a real enthusiasm and knowledge of food and has a passion for cooking and learning, they may be just the one to take on for a trial period. He or she may just have that creative side that those with certificates lack.

Interview objectives
◆ To decide if the applicant is suitable for the job or how suitable the job is for the applicant.
◆ To decide if the applicant will fit into the existing team and the organisation.
◆ To get across the essential expectations and requirements of the job. The interview can be seen as part of the induction process.
◆ To gather information, evaluate it and make a judgement.
◆ To find out the applicant's skills, experience and character.
◆ To assess the interest of the applicant in the business.

Ask open questions, not ones that can only result in a 'yes' or a 'no'. For example:

- ◆ Tell me about your present job.
- ◆ What do you enjoy most about your job?
- ◆ Can you give me some examples?
- ◆ What did you enjoy about college?
- ◆ What made you decide to apply for the job?
- ◆ How do you find dealing with staff?
- ◆ Have you ever dealt with an uncooperative employee? What was the outcome?
- ◆ How do you feel about moving to this part of the country?
- ◆ How will this affect your home life?

◆ TIP ◆

When interviewing staff, ask for references and follow them up.

During the interview

Do get across to potential staff the kind of high standards you expect from them including dress, cleanliness (are those nails and shoes clean?), behaviour (fag breaks are few and far between, for example, and not within eyesight of customers, either inside or out). Their flexibility (can they be called upon to do shifts at short notice?), their attitude to customers and the necessity of teamwork should also be discussed.

Find out if they are familiar with the type of food on offer and are willing to learn. Do they understand about wine and drinks service? If not, are they keen to find out? Can they work under pressure? With a smile? Are they motivated? Do they like working as part of a team? Do they look at you in the eye?

You may sense that they are only working for the money and will be out of the door when the shift ends, not willing to add to the harmony and efficiency of the business if further tidying up, for example, is necessary to be carried out.

Do you in turn give the impression of good management and organisation? Do you offer a decent wage according to experience and skills? Do you come across as a caring person who staff can come to in times of need? Are you approachable? Do you give enough information about your staff needs and expectations? Or will you spring something on them that wasn't mentioned in interview after they have started working for you? You should offer a clear, concise contract with hours, duties and pay structure.

If an employee is to respond to customers' needs they must know:

◆ What the product or service is: its full breadth and its limits.
◆ What the business can do and cannot do: false promises to staff can end in tears and recrimination.
◆ The safeguarding of the organisation: how to be sensitive and discreet about their place of employment.

Make sure you give this information to the employee and that it is not found out by chance. Careful role definition and training is a necessity.

OTHER EMPLOYMENT TIPS

Draw up a job description

No matter how simple or low-level the job, the more information you put down, the better your chances of getting the right person for the job. Cover areas such as skills needed, any training if necessary and how much experience and responsibility the job requires.

Always take up references

Before someone joins your business, ensure you get references. For a fuller, more in-depth reply, phone the referee and ask questions such as 'Would you re-employ this person?'

Make your employees feel welcome

First impressions count and the first three months of employment with a new boss, new colleagues and work is very important. Make your new employee feel welcome. Don't just pass by and say, 'Are you all right?' Spend a few minutes with them to find out if they are feeling included, and if the job is giving them difficulties or pleasure and satisfaction. Give praise where it is due. Keep a list of their birthdays and either wish them happy birthday or give them a card (if the business isn't too huge to handle this act of kindness).

If you run a small business you will be closer to your staff, suppliers and customers than larger ones. Involve your employees in the work culture from day one and keep them up to date with the progress of the business and especially any developments that may take place in the future. Finding out from a third party can lead to disenchantment.

◆ TIP ◆

A business is only as good as the people who work for it.

Staff meals

One of the worst signals you can give your staff is to palm them off with a poor meal while on duty. What is says to them is that you don't place value on them. And how else will they learn about the food they are preparing and serving if they aren't offered it? They will have much more respect for you if given a meal that is nourishing, delicious and shared by all.

◆ EXPERIENCE ◆

Jill Dupleix, The *Times'* newspaper cook and author, passed by London's Kensington Place restaurant and spied staff sitting down to huge bowls of penne with meatballs and a green salad.

Another meal at Zilli Fish in Covent Garden, was equally admired by Jill as staff ate a roasting tray of fat sardines sizzling in garlic and tomatoes, spaghetti with a chilli sauce and roasted red peppers and chicken thighs with a pizzaiola-style sauce.

It doesn't have to cost the earth. Quite the reverse, as demonstrated by those simple dishes. A good meal helps to create a happier team. And if waiting staff eat some of the dishes on the menu they will be better prepared to enthuse about it to guests having also understood the cooking process.

The above examples highlight restaurants, but the same applies to catering. I feel passionately that caterers should feed their staff well. It was one reason for my staff feeling included and well looked after, not just another cog in the wheel. I loved their awakening to different foods and styles of cooking. They were able to describe the food in more detail to customers who in turn felt confident about the ethos of the business. However altruistic this may seem it also helps them to broaden their outlook and to feel part of a strong team.

♦ TIP ♦

Factor in this expense when calculating costs for a catering job.

Appraise your staff regularly

Include a review system for each staff member. The business may have changed, perhaps creating more work for your staff. They may be finding it difficult to absorb without a dip in quality and service. Discuss any issues with the full team present.

Enforce strict 'absence' procedures

In order to deal effectively with absenteeism and late arrival at work, staff should be very clear about company policy. A staff handbook is an ideal way to state policies clearly, even if it is done on an in-house computer rather than going to the expense of printing it.

Areas such as holidays, sickness, absenteeism, lateness, dress code, make-up, jewellery, hair colour, type of shoes, smoking policy and using mobile phones at work should be included and clearly outlined.

Casual labour

Casual labour – staff who work for one-off occasions – are a great resource. Sometimes it can be very useful to employ family and friends. When agreeing to employ someone make sure you set the boundaries. These include:

♦ the time to be at the venue;
♦ how long their services will be required;

◆ work involved;
◆ cleanliness;
◆ dress, hair and jewellery code;
◆ payment per hour and any overtime payment;
◆ travel expenses.

Also, be sure to clarify the final hour of completing a job: the function may be over but there is plenty of washing up, clearing away, stacking, wiping down, sweeping, carrying and loading to do. If they can't commit to any of these requirements, find someone else. A poor staff member can ruin a perfectly good function and will be noticed by the client.

Safeguard your business even if it makes you unpopular with certain family members! You may also find some of them see the job as learning a good, honest trade, even if it is temporary and not their chosen path in life. Waiting skills and a pleasing manner go far in today's world to earn extra cash.

OVERTIME

If you need extra cover for a job, you may make a couple of phone calls to staff and arrange for some overtime. Simple. But overtime can run out of control. Firstly, it can undermine quality of service and secondly, it can undermine recruitment.

For example, people like to earn more but tiredness can, and does, set in. Patterns of good work become just getting by, with staff going through the motions and taking short cuts.

The longer the vacancy exists for that extra staff member, the more existing staff get used to the extra money. When recruitment does take place and a new member joins the team, he or she may be resented as wages decrease for those on overtime.

Be aware and take action if a new member of staff is required to be taken on so that overtime doesn't spiral out of control. Its by-product will be a lowering of standards and creeping inefficiency.

Overtime and paying casual staff

Agree on payment by the hour with both casual and permanent staff before an event. If casual, they will expect to be paid in cash or by cheque when the work is finished. Make sure you keep a record of any overtime undertaken by permanent staff so that there are no disputes when paying.

Agency staff will ask you to fill in a form to ensure that a) you have been happy with everyone's work b) agree to the hours to be paid and c) you have noted any extras: transport, for example. The agency will send you their invoice.

EMPLOYERS' RESPONSIBILITIES

When employing people the first thing to do is to call the New Employers' Helpline on 0845 607 0143. The advisor will set up an employment record and send an Employer's Starter Pack with all information you need. Or you can arrange help from a business advisor from a local Business Support Team.

All services are free and you can also attend one of the local workshops on payroll. Phone them or via www.inlandrevenue.gov.uk/bst/index.htm.

As an employer you are responsible for these areas:

◆ Working out the tax and National Insurance contributions due each pay day.
◆ Keeping accurate and up-to-date records to back up any deduction in your accounts for wages, payments, benefits and such like relating to your employees.
◆ Making payments of Statutory Sick and Maternity pay to your employees as appropriate.
◆ Making Student Loan deductions from an employee's earnings when directed by the Inland Revenue.
◆ Paying Tax Credits to employees when directed by the Inland Revenue.
◆ Paying deductions made over to the Inland Revenue Accounts Office each month – or quarterly if your average monthly payments are below £1,500 – after offsetting any tax credit payments.

◆ At the end of the tax year (April 5) telling the Inland Revenue how much each of your employees has earned and how much tax and NIC (National Insurance Contributions) deductions you have made. You must also give details of any expenses paid or benefits provided to your employees.

Useful telephone numbers and websites:
◆ Help with PAYE (pay as you earn) and/or NIC (national insurance contributions) for New Employers (0845 60 70 143)
◆ National Minimum Wage Helpline (0845 600 0678)
◆ Employers' orderline for forms and stationery orders (08457 646 646)
◆ Useful leaflets and pamphlets via www.inlandrevenue.gov.uk.

The law on pay and hours of work

Legislation is based on British labour law and European social policy for working hours and minimum pay levels, the focus being on:

◆ limiting working hours;
◆ protection from pressure to work excessive hours;
◆ guaranteed holiday pay;
◆ guaranteed rest periods;
◆ guaranteed minimum pay.

National minimum wage

An employer must pay a general minimum rate of at least:

◆ £5.05 an hour for workers over 22 years old;
◆ £4.25 an hour for workers aged 18–21 and for workers aged 22 or over for six months after starting a new job with a new employer and receiving accredited training;
◆ £3 an hour for youth workers: 16-17 years of age.

These rates took effect on 1 October 2005. For more information look at www.tiger.gov.uk.

Working time and pay regulations

An employer must not:

◆ require workers or employees to work more than an average of 48 hours a week, though workers and employees may choose to work longer;
◆ make unauthorised deductions from wages including complete non-payment.

An employer must:

◆ limit the normal working hours of night workers to an average of eight hours in any 24-hour period;
◆ provide all employees with an individual written pay statement at or before the time of payment (under the Employment Rights Act 1996). It must show gross pay and take-home pay with amounts and reasons for variable and fixed deductions. Or, fixed deductions can be shown as a total sum, provided a written statement of these items is given in advance to each employee at least once a year.

In addition, employees have an entitlement to daily, weekly and in-work rest and four weeks' paid annual leave.

Part-time workers' regulations

This is very relevant to the catering business where many staff members are part-timers. Unfortunately, the regulations are poorly adhered to, but they say that part-time employees are not to be treated less favourably than full-time employees, their contractual terms and conditions equal in pay, pensions, annual holidays and training. For further information go to www.dti.gov.uk/er/ptime.htm.

Employing foreign nationals

Nationals of the following new member states of the European Economic Area (EEA) have been free to come to the UK to work from 1 May 2004: Poland, Lithuania, Estonia, Latvia, Slovenia, Slovakia, Hungary and the Czech Republic. Nationals who find a job are required to register with the Home Office under the new Worker Registration Scheme as soon as they find work.

If they plan to work for more than one month for a UK employer they need to register. Once they have been working legally in the UK for 12 months without a break, they will have full rights of free movement.

Those from Austria, Belgium, Cyprus, Italy, Liechtenstein, Denmark, Finland, France, Germany, Greece, Iceland, Ireland, Malta, Netherlands, Norway, Spain and Sweden have been able to work freely in the UK since membership of the EEA.

Nationals from Cyprus and Malta have full free movement rights and are not required to obtain a workers registration certificate.

Many Australians, New Zealanders, Canadians and other Commonwealth nationals come to Britain to work, with a good number of them working in the restaurant trade. Under the Working Holidaymakers Scheme, 17–30 year olds may work in Britain for two years. They may work full- or part-time and can apply once only. They must have the stamp or endorsement clearly marked on their passport for the employer to check.

◆ TIP ◆

For a full list of Commonwealth members and for other information regarding employing foreign nationals, get 'Comprehensive Guidance for United Kingdom Employers on Changes in the Law on Preventing Illegal Working' from www.ind.homeoffice.gov.uk. It can be downloaded. Or call the Employers' Helpline on 0845 010 6677 for a booklet.

If you have employed a foreign national, the way to obtain a National Insurance number is for them to attend an 'evidence of identity' interview at the nearest job centre, taking with them their passport or proof of identity as well as evidence that they are working. For further details contact www.workingintheuk.gov.uk.

Maternity rights

Many stories are carried by the media on the flouting of the laws concerning pregnant employees. Avoid causing a legal hassle by following the points below.

◆ Employers are required to protect the health and safety of employees who are pregnant, have recently given birth or are breast-feeding. (These protections start as soon as the employee is pregnant.)
◆ The contract of employment throughout the 18 weeks' ordinary maternity leave or any additional leave must be continued unless either party to the contract ends it or it expires.
◆ During maternity leave the employee should continue to receive all her contractual benefits except wages.
◆ An employer must not dismiss an employee or select her for redundancy in preference to other comparable employees during her pregnancy or maternity leave just because she is pregnant.

For further information: www.dti.gov.uk/er/maternity.htm.

Redundancy payment

An employer who dismisses an employee by reason of redundancy is required to make a lump sum payment to the employee based on his or her age, length of service and rate of pay at the time of dismissal.

For further information contact 0870 1502 500 or the Department of Trade and Industry's website: www.dti.gov.uk/regs.

Unfair dismissal

Employees who believe they have been unfairly dismissed can complain to an employment tribunal, generally subject to a qualifying period of one year's continuous service. Complaints can be made regardless of length of service if the dismissal is for certain specified reasons, e.g. pregnancy or maternity leave.

Trade union membership

All employees have a right to belong, or not belong, to a trade union. It is unlawful to refuse a person employment because he or she either is or is not a member of a trade union. It is also unlawful for employees to be dismissed or discriminated against because of their membership or non-membership of a trade union.

KITCHEN HIERARCHY

This information applies to larger catering companies but is of interest too to the sole trader. So it is useful if you are new to the business, and also wish to expand into a large catering company.

The professional kitchen's cooking staff are known as the brigade. Like many kitchen words, it comes from the French and, further back, *brigata*, from the Italian, a company or crew, its origins a military one. Look up the word in an Italian dictionary and, ironically, you'll find it comes from the verb *brigare*, 'to brawl, wrangle or fight'.

The size of the brigade is dependent on the establishment. Many small restaurants are based on a head chef, a sous chef and/or a commis chef plus, hopefully, a kitchen porter whose job is mainly to wash up.

Or the staff may be simply the chef, relying on waiting staff to help out with washing up and lesser preparations like plating desserts, prepping breads, butter and ancillaries.

Large restaurants and catering companies have an executive chef, head chef, senior and junior sous ('sous' literally means 'under' in French) chefs, chefs de partie (those responsible for a section of the kitchen such as sauces, larder, starters, mains, vegetables and desserts), demi-chefs de partie (literally 'half'), commis (first and second) chef. A commis, deputy or clerk, learns his or her trade from the bottom of the hierarchy. They are there to help, learn and watch.

There may also be (although it's rare) a chef tournant – an all-purpose chef who is capable of covering all sections and who may be filling in for absent/holidaying chefs.

Definitions: from the lowest to the highest rank
Kitchen porter
Have respect for the KP, as they are affectionately known. Their job is an unenviable one of washing pots, utensils, glasses, plates – the lot – and they may also be offered the joys of prepping vegetables and washing salads. Be

kind to the kitchen porter as he or she must endure repetitive tasks, which are the underpinning of the system.

Commis chef

OK, not the dream job envisaged by some but this is the job to learn by. Duties may include plating up garnishes for all courses with some cooking involved including stocks. Depending on the size of the restaurant, they may deal with stock-taking and deliveries.

Demi chef de partie

This is the next step up: running a station with more responsibilities. It is time for the chef to prove him or herself and showing a willingness to learn and work.

Chef de partie

Literally 'head of a team', the next quasi-military full rank up with the ability to organise other chefs. This is a managerial step up. In a small restaurant a chef de partie may be in charge of just one chef or several in a large one. Duties could include staff meals, sauces, meat and fish prep, hot starters.

Sous chef

This is the head chef's immediate number two and is capable of doing the head chef's job in his or her absence. In a larger kitchen there may be a junior or senior sous chef, a smaller one just the sous (under or sub) chef.

In a big kitchen, the sous chef does little cooking due to managing the kitchen, people, office work, rotas, food ordering, training: it is a position of authority. A junior sous chef is part chef, part manager.

Head chef

In a small restaurant, the head chef is responsible for all cooking, ordering, management and training. The head chef in any size kitchen is in charge. His or her only superior is the executive head chef who may be in charge of several restaurants, either independent ones or within a large company or establishment such as a hotel.

The head chef's jobs are to create menus, write the recipes or guidelines to go with the recipes, find the best suppliers, recruit, discipline and promote staff. In the absence of a sous chef, he or she is also responsible for rotas, giving out specific jobs such as larder work, cleaning, cooking, management, and making sure the kitchen is up to scratch for hygiene and health inspections.

He or she is also responsible for reporting to overall management, discussing future strategies, any special holiday catering such as Christmas or weddings, banqueting, dealing with customer and staff issues and stock-taking checks. Liaison with front of house staff may be delegated to the sous chef.

THE KITCHEN CAREER

Depending on the type of job offered and sought after, working in a restaurant/hotel/catering company kitchen can take many directions. For a commis chef, who has a goal and has to work through a tough time, it can seem insuperable, but under a good head chef this period of learning is worth it.

A commis working for a small business is part of a small brigade and works in all stations. He or she may learn more quickly – and well – if the head chef is good and eager to pass on knowledge and expertise.

In large cities and in a large restaurant/hotel/catering company a commis chef might find the whole process more daunting due to the sheer numbers in the kitchen, and will stay only if given the right treatment in the establishment. But they can move on to other restaurants crying out for staff at this level – and will – if the money and treatment is better.

The fast track to learning in the business is to be a commis in a good, small restaurant/hotel/catering company with maybe four or five chefs, and to be introduced to all stages of cooking. Finding commis chefs who are willing to learn and committed to the job is of paramount importance, in particular to the small- or medium-sized restaurant.

Financially, it is not viable to have several chefs of the same ranking unless business is booming, hence the importance of a keen (and less well paid) commis chef. But do see beyond the cooking skills when interviewing for this position (as described in the section on interviewing staff). The right attitude is of equal importance.

Women chefs

Who says they can't take the pace? There is this myth around – circulated by misogynists – that women aren't strong enough, can't stand the bad language and have an unfortunate attitude to getting on in the kitchen. They cry a lot, they can't lift heavy stock pots, they are moody because of their periods. They can't stand the pace and get flustered easily. Poppycock!

Women have a lot to prove – still – in this male-dominated trade. Many are perceived as being only good as pastry chefs. The discrimination is still quite breath-taking. This is perhaps why I opened and ran a restaurant for eight years in Sussex as chef/owner rather than work for unsympathetic, bullying characters. Of course it is a demanding job but we women can hack it, and offer many good traits, attention to detail being just one.

Witness head chefs Sally Clarke (Clarke's), Angela Hartnett (The Connaught), Ruth Rogers and Rose Gray (River Café), Samantha Clark (Moro), Helena Poulakka (Sonny's), all London-based. And Sonia Brooke-Little, Churchill Arms, Paxford, Gloucestershire, and Shirley Spear and Isobel Tomlin at the Three Chimneys, Isle of Skye. They represent some of the many excellent women head chefs in Britain. For the most part, they are too busy to constantly shout about their prowess in the kitchen.

Caterers of both sexes work in the business with many small companies run by women. There is no sex barrier or age barrier.

KITCHEN AND WAITING STAFF WORKING TOGETHER

Management is responsible for getting the relationship balance right or, at least, recognising the differing tensions within these two groups and settling any disputes and grievances that can build up.

The old adage that the customer is always right can be challenged here when it comes to food. When it is ready, it is at its peak condition and should be served immediately. But large parties can be notoriously difficult to get to sit down at their respective tables. When this happens, communication is extremely vital between these two groups.

For example, the waiter judges the timing of each table and reports back to the kitchen if diners are taking an inordinate amount of time over the first course, for example. Or, conversely, if faster service is required.

◆ TIP ◆

A mutual respect must be built up between kitchen and waiting staff.

If the latter doesn't understand the former's work pattern and degree of skill in putting each dish together then trust, confidence and ability to communicate effectively breaks down.

This is where management comes in and should be aware of tension building up. Turn the tables and get them to perform each other's work or at least shadow different sections to understand their challenges and difficulties.

STAFF BEHAVIOUR

Your waiting and kitchen staff reflect the kind of catering company you are running. Therefore, make sure of the following.

Appearance

If staff have a uniform, make sure it is clean, pressed, uniform in style and well-fitting. If you operate a no-uniform policy, then stipulate what your staff should wear and be vigilant as to the characteristics as mentioned above. Do stipulate too the type of shoes, that they should be in good repair and cleaned regularly, and the policy on the wearing of jewellery, make-up, style of hair. I am totally opposed to any jewellery apart from a simple wedding ring and instruct staff to remove any jewellery including ear or nose studs. The same goes for too much make-up, an elaborate hairstyle and haircombs.

Hygiene

All staff should have short, clean, unvarnished nails and must wash their hands after a fag break, going to the loo or returning to duty after going to the shops, handling stock from a van, etc.

All of the above applies too to kitchen staff. The cleanliness of their aprons, chefs' jackets and the wearing of head gear are of paramount importance not only to the overall standards of hygiene but also if seen by clients and guests (these are possible future clients after all) who will judge the business accordingly.

No kitchen clothing such as chefs' jackets should be worn outside the premises as it could introduce dirt and germs on return into the kitchen.

Smoking

Smoking is a vexed question in the catering trade as there is a high ratio of smokers to non-smokers, who simply can't live without a fag break.

◆ Be strict about fag breaks as it is unfair on the non-smokers who have to pick up the slack.
◆ Make sure that smokers are not seen by clients or guests hovering by an open door or by the bins as this really does give a wrong impression.
◆ All smokers should wash their hands before service. If there is an all-pervading smell of smoke it can be a real turn-off for the customer (smoky clothes, breath, hands).

◆ TIP ◆

Banning smoking by staff can be tantamount to calling for a mutiny. You may be fortunate enough to employ non-smokers but, if not, be a vigilant manager/owner.

Drugs

If you suspect any staff member has a drug problem, deal with it. If they come in late, don't turn up at all or show signs of drug and alcohol abuse, do you really want this kind of behaviour in your business? No.

SERVICE

A good waiting staff member is able to relate to clients' and guests' needs. Self-respect and respect of others is paramount as is professionalism and efficiency. A good memory is also important.

Make sure waiting staff know what the chosen menu is and if there are any special dietary requirements that have been pre-ordered by the client.

Waiting staff must not only be aware of what the dishes consist of but also the wines they are serving. They should be knowledgeable about all the drinks on offer. It should not be just guesswork on their part. What kind of coffee do you buy? What is the wine being served?

Waiting staff should make sure that there is sufficient space on the table before serving plates, vegetables, wine bottles, butter, bread and other items. It's no good just pushing things around the table to fit them in, as it creates tension with the guest and a feeling of not being looked after appropriately. A kind of take it or leave it attitude.

Lasting impressions: dos and don'ts

All staff should say goodbye as warmly as when they greeted guests on arrival. This will create a lasting impression.

- Don't fawn or ingratiate yourself or be over-familiar.
- Don't be loud or noisy.
- Don't ever, ever be rude.
- Do be friendly, pleasant, efficient and professional.

Tips for professional waiting skills

- Serve from the left and remove from the right.
- Hold the plate by placing four fingers under it, with the thumb on the side and not on the surface of the plate.
- When holding two plates in one hand, balance one plate on the forearm by the wrist, with three fingers under the top plate, thumb and small finger on the rim of the lower plate.
- Clear plates by balancing one plate as above for cutlery, the stronger part of the forearm and wrist bearing the weight of the cleared plates.

- Serve drinks on the right where the glass is positioned.
- Always hold glasses by their stem, never the bowl.
- Clear the table after each course, leaving it set for the next course.
- Always make sure the table is left cleared ready for dessert or coffee with the removal of salt and pepper and unnecessary cutlery, for example.
- Clear plates only when everyone at a table has finished eating. It is gives the wrong impression, i.e. you're hurrying them, if cleared at different times, making the slower eater at the table feel awkward.

Management skills

A good caterer shows self-confidence, has a complete understanding of the operation, maintains a good rapport between catering staff, client and guests and possesses charm.

He or she is a leader, takes responsibility and can delegate well but must also be able to be hands-on without undermining other staff, e.g. showing them up before clients, guests and other staff members.

The same dos and don'ts apply too to the caterer as well as to waiting staff (see dress code, smoking, behaviour and service above).

STAFF ROTAS

Rotas are a vital tool for any catering company, large or small. At a glance, everyone can see who is working or having time off. They are made up on a weekly basis but, with good management and knowledge of all the catering jobs, they can be worked out several weeks ahead of time, taking into consideration holidays, days off, staff shortages, overtime or busy times of year with more staff required.

It is important to put your managerial skills into practice here and be as fair to all staff members as possible. For example, unless specifically asked for, don't pile all the evening work on some staff members. Give them equal numbers of day shifts as their co-workers so they have a night off with their family and friends.

> ◆ **TIP** ◆
>
> Discuss the rota with all staff and follow up any complaints or dissatisfaction promptly as grievances can build up.

Include cleaning and refrigeration temperature checking too on staff rotas so that they are brought to the forefront. They should be seen as a necessary part of the working week, not just something to be fitted in as and when, or done in a desultory fashion, or even forgotten.

Print out staff rotas and preferably re-print if there are a number of changes so that confusion doesn't arise. Otherwise, a member of staff may not turn up, mistakenly thinking that he or she had swapped duties.

Below is an example of a staff rota for a small catering company.

Staff	Tuesday	Wednesday	Thursday	Friday	Saturday	Sunday
Annie: co-owner	8am–8pm	10am–6pm	off	9am–2pm 6pm–11pm	4pm–11pm	10am–6pm
Charlie: co-owner	off	10am–6pm	9am–6pm	10am–2pm 6pm–11pm	11am–7pm	10am–4pm
KP 1 Kay	off	10am–6pm	off	9am–5pm	10am–6pm	off
KP 2 Andy	9am–6pm	off	9am–5pm	5pm–11pm	off	9am–5pm
Alice	off	11am–4pm	10am–2pm	6pm–11pm	5pm–12pm	11am–5pm
Bill	off	off	off	10am–2pm 6pm–11pm	10am–2pm 6pm–1pm	11am–5pm

CLEANING

Cleaning is an essential part of any food business. It minimises the risk of food contamination and infestation, and provides a pleasant and safe working environment.

To be effective, cleaning must be planned and incorporated into the staff rota.

◆ Adopt a clean-as-you-go policy with spillages and food debris when preparing food.
◆ Draw up a list of all items of equipment and areas for cleaning and how often they need to be cleaned.
◆ Compile a separate list for toilet maintenance and cleaning.
◆ Specify what materials and equipment need to be used for equipment and areas.
◆ Also specify who is responsible for these jobs.
◆ Prepare a comprehensive scheduled programme.
◆ Review the programme if there is a new piece of equipment or a new area.
◆ Store cleaning materials away from all food.
◆ Keep cleaning materials in their original containers.
◆ Don't mix cleaning materials as noxious fumes can be given off.
◆ Wash hands after using any cleaning materials.

Staff to guest ratio
◆ Formal seated buffet/dinners: one waiting staff per ten guests.
◆ Drinks parties: one bar person and three waiting staff per 50 guests.
◆ Fork buffet parties: one bar person and two waiting staff per 30 guests.
◆ Afternoon tea: two waiting staff per 30 guests.

BRIEFING WAITING STAFF

Staff should arrive two hours before a large function such as a buffet or dinner to set up and to be given a briefing. Staff should stay for at least half an hour after the last guest has left so that all clearing up can take place. For a drinks party, depending on the size, ask staff to come an hour to an hour and a half before guests are due to arrive.

It is important to be clear and to brief them when they arrive. Tell them:

◆ the timings for guests' arrival, meal service and expected end of event;
◆ the number of guests;

- the menu and any special catering requirements such as vegetarian, vegan, gluten-free, dairy-free meals and who they are for;
- the drinks and wines to serve (or to keep replenishing the tables for guests to help themselves);
- any special wishes of the client for the table (e.g. place name cards);
- where all the equipment is to be found and what to do with dirty plates etc on clearing;
- where coffee and tea is to be served (in reception area or at the table?);
- where coats and hats are stored;
- where staff can leave their belongings;
- where the toilets are;
- what the staff will have to eat and when to take a break.

Remind them to:

- set up the bar and tables;
- clear ashtrays and replace them;
- clear pre-dinner drinks and nibbles from the reception area;
- clear the dining room, reception and kitchen areas, including the washing up and putting away, at the end of the function.

◆ TIP ◆

When catering for a large function, I always have the basics of the event written up and attached to a board for staff to read after the briefing to refresh their memory.

When hiring staff, provide a meal if they are working for four hours or more. It is standard practice for the client to pay for a taxi home if the party finishes after buses and tubes have stopped for the night.

13

Keeping Your Business on Track

You're up and running and your catering business is now starting to take off but there are still teething problems. This chapter deals with:

◆ solving business problems;
◆ keeping costs down;
◆ reducing risk;
◆ keeping those vital customers.

One satisfying part of your business is solving catering problems for your customers. You offer them a solution and if it works well it will earn you bonus points when they need the services of a catering company for future events.

Of course you won't be able to satisfy every customer's needs. You won't always be the right company for them.

If you are not able to solve a particular customer's needs (for example, you were unable to supply a company a Thai buffet lunch for 30 at short notice), ask yourself why and if you can address their wishes in the future. Perhaps next time you could offer different food, or offer the whole package from food, staffing, marquee and equipment hire to flowers, the band and finding a good toastmaster?

Remember, however, that although you don't want the business to go to a competitor, you can't always give every customer what they need. Accept your limitations.

KEEPING YOUR CUSTOMERS

When a function is over, talk to your customer. Ask them if there are any improvements that you could make, especially if you do business with them on a regular basis (daily, weekly) or you are in contract catering, providing a daily in-house catering service for a business, for example. If you take the time to talk, they may also suggest other businesses or private customers who are looking for a good, reliable caterer.

Questions to ask existing customers
- Do you have other events coming up you need catering for?
- Can we give you a quote?
- What other services can we offer you? What else are you looking for?
- Are you pleased with our standards or can we improve on our existing service to you?

EFFECTIVE TIME SCHEDULING

Some one-man band businesses fail because they can't work out how to use time effectively. Try the following to help you manage your time.

- **Prioritise your workload** in a sensible way. Do the jobs you need to do first. Don't put them off because you can't face them.

- ◆ **Make a list** which includes most important, and least important.
- ◆ **Work through your list of food preparation** effectively. For example, if something takes a long time to bake then start preparing other smaller dishes that need less time while that item is baking. If you use the oven a lot, make a list of items that need to be baked first.
- ◆ **Do as much shopping as you can** in one go so that you can work through a lot of food preparation without having to go out to buy missing items.
- ◆ **Keep up to date with invoice payments** so that you don't run into a cash-flow problem.
- ◆ **Communicate well** with your employees, and with your family, so that efficiency and good relationships reign.

SOLVING BUSINESS PROBLEMS

Catering throws up daily problems which can affect the growth of your business as well as your satisfaction and success. It is part and parcel of being in this business and dealing with problems is, without doubt, a skill you need. Think about how you would deal with the following:

- ◆ Your refrigeration stops functioning and you need to sort it out – fast.
- ◆ A key staff member has to go to a family funeral at short notice, on the day of a large function.
- ◆ The 60 chicken breasts you ordered are preposterously small – your new supplier has let you down with only 24 hours to go until the party.
- ◆ You lose a catering job you thought you had.
- ◆ A customer is dissatisfied with the wine you supplied.
- ◆ You are late for a function due to a faulty vehicle.
- ◆ There are ten extra guests and no extra food.
- ◆ The hired-in tablecloths haven't been laundered properly and there are holes in several of them.
- ◆ Your landlord is demanding a rent increase.
- ◆ Your customer's personal assistant is undermining you and creating a division between you and the client.

Problems arise for many reasons: bad management or a short-sighted view of your business, or things out of your control such as staff absence or mechanical problems like fridge breakdown. It's all part of the human condition and some things are not instantly solvable but, with practice and experience, you can get around them temporarily.

Whatever the situation, keep a cool head as stress will only compound the problem. You must learn how to deal with problems logically, rationally and with the utmost good humour even in trying circumstances. Trust your intuition. It comes from your knowledge, experience and reality.

Long-term problems

If there are long-term problems that need careful analysis rather than instant patching up, have a brainstorming session with those who you trust and whose input you value: partners (a must), staff, family, friends, accountant, solicitor, bank manager.

It isn't possible to foresee all problems so don't be too hard on yourself. But once you recognise that a long-term problem exists, ask some pertinent questions:

◆ What are the full facts of the problem?
◆ When has this happened before and why is it happening again?
◆ Is this an internal or external problem?
◆ Is it causing conflict? How?
◆ Is it affecting my business short or long term?
◆ Is it affecting employees? My family? My health?
◆ How can I plan ahead so that this doesn't happen again?
◆ Is it due to bad habits, rash decisions, procrastination?

Analyse causes of the problem and possible solutions. For example, if you tend to forget to pack certain items for an event, is it due to poor list-keeping and checking before leaving or are you not thinking out the whole event from A to Z? Are your administration skills in dire need of an overhaul so that you can find all the necessary paperwork quickly and when needed?

Solutions and action

Make a list and discard those ideas that just won't work. Get feedback from those who you've drawn into your brainstorming circle. They may be able to throw light on how cost-effective the solution is or how impractical it is time-wise. Consider the following:

◆ Who will be involved in solving this problem? How?
◆ What is the outcome I expect?
◆ When should I start the plan of action? Where? How?
◆ What is the cost involved? Or can it be solved without financial output?

REDUCING RISK

You may have increased your business turnover and managed to get costs down, but your business stability can still be jeopardised by the following:

◆ personal injury;
◆ not putting aside enough profits for paying taxes;
◆ food spoilage (and no insurance to cover it);
◆ legal problems (food poisoning, an employee sues you);
◆ lack of profitable catering jobs;
◆ bad debts;
◆ fire and flood;
◆ theft, vandalism, vehicle accidents;
◆ poor management practices;
◆ asset problems;
◆ your landlord ousting you from the premises;
◆ alcoholism;
◆ partnership difficulties due to incompatibility, illness, disability or death.

Although easier said than done, the best way to reduce these and other risks is to be aware of them before they happen. Constantly analyse your management, make sure you have sufficient insurance and never forget the marketing side of your business which may need to be re-addressed if business is slack.

Try to stay one step ahead. Take some time to think:

◆ What could cause a loss to my business?
◆ How serious could this loss be?

Theft and vandalism

Are your premises, including any outbuildings, secure enough to avoid theft and vandalism? These problems can be due to petty thievery (drug-related crimes) and just sheer acts of destruction for the sake of it. On two occasions, my outbuilding has been broken into (once even hacking through the roof!) with disastrous food-spoilage and theft. Enlist the help of your local police crime officer for valuable advice. And heed it.

Personal injury

Obviously, personal injury is a problem if you are the sole caterer. You may be able to get around this short-term by taking on an employee or you may be fortunate enough to have good friends and family who can cook well. When I broke my arm, excellent friends rallied around to cook. I was able to advise from the side, and this literally saved my bacon. You may be able to insure for cover, depending on your circumstances, so do shop around for an insurance quote.

Fire and flood

Losing catering records by fire or flood is a calamity, making it difficult to send out outstanding invoices and pay your bills. Food preparation may become impossible, and your business may face temporary closure. Look out for business interruption insurance that can tide you over should you be affected.

Reducing risk is also achieved by experience and you will learn as time goes by to do your job faster, more efficiently and more profitably. Talk to other food businesses to gain further knowledge on risk reduction. You can help each other by sharing good advice.

Contact local and national associations such as the Enterprise Centre, Business Link, National Business Advice Service and other organisations (see Chapter 5 on business) for advice before starting your business. There are many seminars, discussions and talks you may be able to attend to increase your knowledge, thereby reducing some of these risks.

LONG-TERM SUCCESS FOR YOUR CATERING BUSINESS

Catering, in common with many other businesses, is not a quick fix business. It takes time to achieve your goals. You have to learn how to create a viable business that encompasses good practices in planning, management, and how to deal with customers so that you get the business in the first place.

You will need to be a good negotiator and learn what works in order to get the job. You also need to deal with suppliers, negotiate with staff, family and other people with whom you share your life.

Tips for achieving long-term success

◆ Develop good relationships with existing customers and always try to get new ones.
◆ Develop good relationships with employees, suppliers and others essential to making your business work.
◆ Work as part of a team.
◆ Develop good practices in accountancy and office management.
◆ Constantly look at ways to improve services to customers, and keep abreast of trends and good business practices.
◆ Be aware of time wasting – interruptions, visitors, failure to delegate, lack of self-discipline – and deal with them.
◆ Never lose track of what matters most in your life.
◆ Make sure you have time to get some physical exercise and quality time out. It helps to alleviate stress, allows you to think and keeps you fit for your demanding job.

14

It's Show Time! Running an Event

Finally, you have arrived at the stage when your organisational skills, expertise, professionalism and planning are tested: your first event. This is your chance to show your client that you can measure up to their expectations.

DEALING WITH CRISES

Of course sometimes there are unforeseen disasters. Some things you could not have predicted.

◆ EXPERIENCE ◆

In my 20 years of being a chef, and running a restaurant and a catering business, I can recall many things that could have been prevented, and some that could never have been forecast. Like the time the water sprinklers went off in a posh art gallery. I had been contracted to do the catering for 100 for a major artist's retro-spective. There were dukes, duchesses, the great and good and key media people in attendance.

The fire brigade arrived and charged up the 18th-century staircase past the guests of honour (one of them broadcaster and author David Attenborough), brandishing all manner of fire-fighting gear, to the offending cooker which had caused the problem in the first place. It had overheated a small office which had doubled up as a kitchen. No one needed that extra frisson of excitement. The art and event should have been ample! Needless to say, the gallery and I parted company.

Another time the power failed in a marquee during a charity dinner for 130. The cookers, heating, lights and refrigeration all extinguished. It was on a cold November evening, and the rain was lashing down. Singers couldn't read their music so couldn't perform. Dinner was only partly served. The marquee had been placed on a slope which meant that guests and staff alike almost needed climbing gear to move around. Nightmare scenario.

Moral: talk to the marquee company and the client about the positioning of the marquee, the effectiveness of the electrics and if there is enough power for all the equipment. Don't leave it up to the client, but liaise with them on all arrangements.

I could tell you about many mishaps. But these incidents, although vivid in my memory, are few and far between. The only course of action the caterer can take is to keep a very cool head and try to rectify the situation. (For those of you who like a happy ending: yes, the singers sang and the guests did finish their meal thanks to a call to a local electrician.)

A lot of running a catering business is about experience that you will pick up as you take on more and more jobs. You will learn as your business pro-gresses that certain demands clients have are achievable and that others are impossible. You will get the hang of finding more workable alternatives that mean an event will run smoothly.

PLANNING AHEAD

Even large catering companies such as Party Ingredients, who I mentioned in an earlier chapter, shop for parties on an individual basis rather than buying in wholesale perishable items such as meat, dairy produce and breads.

Of course, you (and they) will have a stock cupboard of condiments, flour, sugar, mustards, honeys, rice, couscous, lentils and other ingredients which are on-going.

Ordering in advance

For a specific party, ordering in advance is essential if it is a large party. It's essential too if you have a small party but the main ingredients are not readily available. Once you have agreed the menu with the client and received the deposit, you can start to order the main items on your list. If your client has requested the best smoked salmon Scotland can offer and stuffed quail or vension, phone your suppliers to order and arrange for delivery or collection.

Compiling the shopping list

The full list of what you need to buy can alter, bearing in mind that numbers can change up to a week before the event. There will be a little fluctuation in the shopping list. I usually list all the dairy produce in one line, the vegetables and fruit in another, dried goods and meat, fish etc in other lines. I am sure you do too when shopping for the household anyway. Just keep these sensible practices in your business. Store this list away in the file you have opened for the client's event.

◆ TIP ◆

> Make sure you have ordered everything the client has asked for in plenty of time: the equipment hire, the cake, the music, the flowers. Have all this confirmed in writing.

Hiring staff

Hire any staff you need as soon as you get the go-ahead from the client. Re-confirm with them a week before the party and give directions to the client's house/business/premises where event is to be held.

Preparing the food

I have a whiteboard in my kitchen which is well-used. I write down all the dishes that need to be prepped and, against them, I put the day they are to be prepared and finished. Work out the approximate time it will take. That final tick against each dish is pleasurable and it is a great help in being able to see your exact workload.

EXAMPLE DINNER PARTY

You have three days to shop and to prepare the following menu for 20 at a party on Friday:

Crab soup with saffron and leek and rolls
Stuffed quail with wild rice and thyme and a port sauce
Pommes Parisienne (little potato balls)
Assorted vegetables
Lemon tart with fresh berries
Coffee served in cafetieres plus mint tea, sugar, milk and chocolate truffles

Wednesday

◆ Shop for most of the ingredients (bar the quail and crab which have been ordered) but leave the herbs, berries and bread items until Friday for freshness.

◆ Store them carefully in the fridge, marked for the specific party if there is food for other parties as well.

Thursday

◆ Collect the quail from the butcher's and the crab from the fishmonger. Or they may deliver.

◆ Start prepping the fish stock for the soup and the chicken stock for the port sauce.

- Prepare the wild rice stuffing and refrigerate.
- Make the lemon tart dough and refrigerate.
- Finish off the Port sauce and refrigerate.

Friday (day of the party)

- Collect the ordered rolls and berries.
- Finish off the soup and place in lidded container for transportation. Label and refrigerate when cool.
- Stuff the quail and place in lidded container. Label and refrigerate when cool.
- Bake blind the lemon tart cases, prep the filling and bake. Cool. Refrigerate. Prepare for transport.
- Prep the potato balls, place in lidded container, cover with water. Refrigerate.
- Prep the vegetables and place in lidded containers. Refrigerate.
- Make a checklist of all items to take:

Food items

butter for glazing the vegetables;
oil for the potatoes;
sea salt and pepper mill;
icing sugar;
fresh mint and berries for decorating the lemon tart;
fresh herbs for chopping for the soup;
crab and leeks to add to the soup;
coffee, tea, sugar, cream, milk;
chocolate truffles.

Non-food items

knives;
ladles;
boards;
sieves;
pans;
whisks;
slices;

cafetieres;

clean apron;

clean cloths;

copy of the menu.

♦ Check you know where you're going. Make sure you have the correct address, map and a telephone number in case you're delayed and need to contact the party giver.

♦ If agreed with the client, take the invoice to be paid or leave it with the client in an envelope. Leave a blank space for the staff hours then add these in and the final total before sealing the envelope.

And finally:

♦ Fill up the chilled cool boxes and containers with your chilled prepared food and equipment and leave in good time for the event.

> **♦ TIP ♦**
>
> Always take a last look around the kitchen and in the fridge. It's all too easy to leave something behind.

MANAGING AN EVENT

This applies to most outside catering events. If you cater for other types of work such as sandwich-making, cooking for a variety of outlets and delivering the food, many of these points will also apply to you.

Timing

You will have discussed with your client and your staff what time you are expected to arrive. If you are catering for a small drinks party or a dinner party, allow $1-1\frac{1}{2}$ hours before the event starts. If you have quite a lot of prepping still to do, or a roast, you may need more time.

For a large party, arrive a good two hours beforehand so that you and your staff can set up the chairs, tables, tablecloths, napkins, side plates, lay cutlery, polish glasses for the bar and get the kitchen ready.

You will want everything in place before guests arrive. The client will feel confident that everything is under control.

Introduce the staff to the host/hostess. Smile. Look relaxed but professional. Don't get into long, involved conversations if possible. You have work to do and they have to finalise their own arrangements and might still have to get dressed for the occasion.

Checking

Go over the planning: when the food is to be served, how the host/ess would like the wine service (are they or a staff member doing it?) and vegetables served (silver service or placed in dishes for guests to help themselves?).

Re-check the table. Make sure it has everything on it (salt and pepper, napkins, water glasses etc). Do the cutlery or glasses need a polish?

Check the plates for each course. Are they big enough? Will you have to use the same plates for each course and wash them up in between courses rather swiftly if they're not the right size? (This applies only to small at-home parties. You will have arranged hire of sufficient plates for a large party in a marquee, for example.)

Do you have the right-sized vegetable dishes, bread container, butter dishes, serving spoons?

◆ TIP ◆

DON'T PANIC! If you have forgotten something, improvise or ask your client if you can 'borrow' some extra milk or gently raid their mint plant for some garnish. Keep calm: act like a professional. Mistakes can happen and there is usually a way around it.

Serving

Liaise with the host/ess before plating up the first course (for at-home dinner parties and formal marquee events). If you are premature your food may spoil. Timing is everything!

Remember to delegate. Your staff must receive instructions from you in order to fulfil their role professionally.

Clearing up

When the last course has gone out and the coffee is being prepared, put yourself or your team to work on the washing up and leave the kitchen as you found it. (Floor and surfaces clean? Sink wiped down?)

Any leftovers should be labelled and refrigerated. Let your client know what you have put in their fridge.

♦ TIP ♦

If you are working in a marquee and the food has been around for a while without refrigeration, I do advise throwing it out to safeguard against food-poisoning.

Check with your client if everything was to their satisfaction before leaving. Check the kitchen one last time for your items, especially if it will be a long way back to collect them.

If you are using casual staff, pay them on leaving. Make sure you have sufficient cash or a chequebook with you. Have they had something to eat and drink? They need to be well looked after too – and thanked for their work.

Remember to look after yourself and your staff. Drink plenty of water, especially at a large function, take a change of shoes to give your feet a break and have a five-minute sit down and some energy-giving food.

AFTER THE EVENT

On return to your premises, unload and put away all the equipment. It will make your kitchen more efficient the following day if you can start from scratch with a tidy, organised kitchen.

Send the invoice in the next couple of days if you haven't left it with the client. Check to see that all receipts and the clients' paperwork have been filed properly so that you can easily locate them if necessary.

> ◆ TIP ◆
>
> Call the client a day or two later to check if they were happy with the catering and arrangements.

Of course, with a larger function, you will need to be doubly organised. If you are catering for a wedding, for example, that needs hire equipment, you will need to check after the event that all the equipment is boxed up and ready for collection by the company before leaving the venue.

You may have been working in a marquee without hot and cold running water, your cooking dishes returning dirty with you to your premises. Soak them overnight if it is too late and you and your staff are too tired to take care of the washing up. There has to be a sensible cut-off point but if you have a busy schedule the following day, you may have to grit your teeth and roll those sleeves up no matter how tired you are.

> ◆ TIP ◆
>
> When catering for a very large party in a marquee where there is no hot or cold running water, make sure that you hire equipment that can be sent back dirty. Otherwise you will be spending far too much energy and time washing up. The same goes if there is an inadequate kitchen, such as in a village hall. Discuss these finer points with your client and impress upon them what is and isn't practical. You must charge for any extra time and employ extra staff if there is no way around it.

BEING A CATERER

Is it worth it? This catering business? Is it too much like hard work or does catering give pleasure and satisfaction not only to you but also to your clients and their guests? You need to be a realist about its pressures and its essential attention to detail.

Being a good cook is just part of the equation. You also need to be a good manager and hone your skills in accountancy and staff delegation. Without a doubt, caterers need to have a remarkable numbers of skills, which are developed along the way, and a drive to succeed. It is mostly great fun, and highly stimulating; it can become your passion.

It is possible to start cooking from a small flat and progress to a large company like Party Ingredients' chef/owner Peter Gladwin has. You may begin, as countless others have done, by cooking, washing up, delivering, doing the accounts, writing menus, dabbling in marketing, finding casual staff, like your mother and your best friend, and planning everything down to the last detail.

Your business may grow from personal recommendation and move into dedicated premises. Or you may prefer to remain a small business with few overheads. Whatever and wherever your business takes you, you will be certain to meet the most fascinating, delightful and demanding people along the way – may it give you much pleasure and a fulfilling lifestyle.

Helpful hints from experienced caterers

- When starting, beware of your own naivety.
- Select staff who wish to make catering their career rather than those just in it for the money.
- Don't select staff who think that because they have been through catering college they know everything. In this business you never stop learning.
- Be realistic and straightforward, avoiding all pretentiousness.
- Don't use your imagination just for the sake of seeming imaginative.
- Only cook what you understand and cook well.
- Buy in small quantities, frequently, so that your food is always fresh.
- If you mix a variety of ingredients from East and West, know what you are doing. It could result in a total mishmash of flavours with customers running screaming from the premises. Pickled ginger with mashed potatoes doesn't work as a pairing.
- Get an accountant!
- Word of mouth is the best advertising. For every satisfied new customer, another five to ten people will hear about it from that customer.
- Be good humoured.
- Have good interpersonal skills.
- Have good feet!
- Be a mind reader.
- Honestly know your food and mind.
- Enjoy company and really like people.
- Hire staff carefully: they need to fit in personally as well as being efficient.
- Create a happy kitchen atmosphere. Don't have chefs who cook in anger. Customers will pick it up.
- The best food is soul food and you can't cook in chaos or that sweaty, macho, it's-hell-in-here-but-we-will-get-the-job-done atmosphere so beloved of catering regiments. Ever notice women don't cook like that?

- Believe in what you are doing and look at the long term.
- Be consistent.
- Raise your prices slowly.
- Do not try to please everyone.
- Know your strengths and weaknesses.
- When starting your business, keep your price below the competition and your quality above.
- It is important to be able to say no.
- Develop your palate. Always try new tastes and keep up to date.
- Never serve food you do not taste.
- Being a caterer can eat up family life. Safeguard your family by spending more time with them. This is vital.
- Service is not servility.
- Encourage children to eat all types of food. They are the next generation.
- It is a mistake to presume that good food alone makes a good catering business.
- Know your market and know who you are catering to then design your menu, premises, ambience, pricing, service, style.
- Regard cooking and service as equally important.
- Lead by example, by training all staff to respect their work and the contribution they make to the business.
- Avoid pushy advertising and salespeople.
- You need to be strong in mind and body, as catering demands are great.
- Be loyal to good suppliers and pay them on time. They will go out of their way to help you in the future.
- Never make drastic changes to the menu but change them gradually and within seasons. Your customers might be put off by too drastic a menu change.
- Be patient with staff. You will rarely have perfect staff so look to their positive points and hope to improve their bad ones. See them blossom.
- Getting the right financial and accounting advice from the beginning is the difference between a viable and non-viable business.
- Keep up with your paperwork. If you can't, hire a bookkeeper.
- Set-up costs can be frightening. Don't be put off. You have to spend money to make money.
- Kitchen equipment can be bought second-hand or leased.

- Market research is important. There is no point in offering your style of cooking if there is no demand.
- Never rest on your laurels.
- Don't be under-financed as the pressure will force you to work all hours.
- Take good breaks to restore the brain and for inspiration.
- Pay attention to detail. It's the little things that matter.

Glossary

Al dente An Italian term meaning 'to the tooth'. To cook pasta so it has a resistance to the bite.

Bain-marie Deep pan of hot water in which dishes to be cooked are placed prior to being put in a low temperature oven. Also a large water tray on top of the stove to keep sauces like Hollandaise and custard warm without overcooking or spoiling.

Bake blind Baking pastry cases without filling, but lined with foil and ceramic or metal beans then baking prior to filling being added.

Blanch/refresh Fast boiling vegetables for a few minutes then refreshing in cold water to keep their colour. A possible holding point for further cooking. Can also be for whitening meats or fish to remove any trace of impurities. Also for skin removal of nuts, tomatoes, peaches and peppers.

Chambrer To bring cheeses to room temperature for maximum flavour.

Clarify butter Removing the milky residue by gently heating butter then either pouring it through muslin or pouring it carefully into a container without disturbing the residue

Confit Traditionally, confit only applied to lightly salted duck or goose cooked slowly in its own fat and then preserved in this fat. When ordered, the meat is then roasted. Nowadays, it is widely misinterpreted on menus, sadly demonstrating the restaurateur's basic lack of knowledge.

Corked wine Wine that has been tainted by a contaminated cork.

Decant Pouring liquid – wine, meat juices etc – carefully from one container to another without disturbing the sediment.

Deglaze Adding liquid – stock or wine – to a pan in which meat has been roasted then boiling to reduce and whisking into the concentrated juices and crusty bits to form a gravy which is then strained and seasoned.

Gratin A preparation of food cooked in a shallow dish with a sauce and finished in the oven or under the grill to produce a crust thanks to the addition of breadcrumbs or cheese.

Julienne Cutting vegetables into strips or matchstick shapes.

Jus Very often misinterpreted, the jus is short for 'jus de viande' (juices of the meat). Nowadays it is a sauce halfway between a gravy and a complex sauce made from stock, wine and other seasonings.

Lardons Small strips of bacon, salt pork or pork fat blanched then sautéed.

Mirin Japanese sweet cooking wine made from fermented rice grains.

Miso A savoury paste of cooked soya beans with grains, yeasted grains and sea salt which is fermented for one or two years.

Monter Whisking cold cubes of butter into a sauce to thicken it. Can also mean whisking egg whites lightly or stiffly.

Quinoa (pronounced 'keen-wha') Gluten-free grain similar to bulgar wheat and used instead of rice, couscous or bulgar for those on a gluten-free diet.

Reduce Reducing a stock or sauce by evaporation over a high heat until it reaches the wished-for consistency. This intensifies the flavours.

Relax Relaxing meat after cooking allows the re-balancing of juices and enhances the colour of red meat.

Roux A mix of fat, usually butter, and flour which is whisked in little by little to thicken a sauce. It must be cooked for quite a while to eliminate the taste of raw flour.

Sautéing Literally 'to jump' (French). The shallow frying of smallish pieces of food in an open pan with fat to brown.

Supreme The skinless breast and wing of chicken or game such as pheasant. It can also be applied to fish fillets to glamorise them on restaurant menus.

Sweat Cooking food over a gentle heat, usually in oil and/or butter, until softened but without colour.

Terrine An ovenproof, usually loaf-shaped, dish for cooking patés with or without a pastry crust.

Tornedos A small, round, usually expensive steak cut from the thickest part of the fillet. Trimmed of all sinew and fat.

Tourner or to turn Cutting vegetables into olive, almond or barrel shapes.

Wilt Usually a green leaf or herb with a few drops of water from its washing and turned with tongs in a hot pan until just wilted but retaining its colour.

Useful contacts

British Chambers of Commerce: www.britishchambers.org.uk

British Hospitality Association: www.bha-online.org.uk or 020 7404 7744

Business Debtline: 0800 197 6026

Business Eye in Wales: www.businessconnect.org.uk or 08457 9697 98

Business Gateway (Scotland-Lowlands): www.bgateway.com or 0845 609 6611

Business Link: 0845 600 9006 or www.businesslink.gov.uk

Campaign for Real Food, PO Box 132, Sutton, SM3 8WQ: 0800 328 3750. www.thecarf.co.uk

Catering Equipment Suppliers' Association, Carlyle House, 235 Vauxhall Bridge Road, London SW1V 1EJ. 020 7233 7724. www.cesa.org.uk

Companies House: www.companies-house.gov.uk or 0870 333 3636

Equal Opportunities Commission: www.eoc.org.uk or 0845 601 5901

Federation of Small Businesses: www.fsb.org.uk

Food Standards Agency – for A–Z of who to contact (from alcoholic drinks to waste issues): 020 7276 8000 or www.foodstandards.gov.uk

Food Standards Agency – for publications: www.food.gov.uk or 0845 606 0667

Food Standards Agency – site for caterers: www.food.gov.uk/cleanup

Health and Safety Executive: www.hse.gov.uk or 08701 545500

Henrietta Green's Food Lovers' Fairs: www.foodloversfairs.com

HM Customs & Excise National Advice Service: 0845 010 9000

Highlands and Islands Enterprise (Scotland-Highlands): www.hie.co.uk

Home Office helpline re overseas workers: 0845 010 6677 or www.ind.homeoffice.gov.uk

Imported Food Helpline: 020 7276 8018 (Food Standards Agency)

Inland Revenue: www.inlandrevenue.gov.uk

Landlord disputes: www.bdl.org.uk

The National Association of Farmers' Markets: www.farmersmarkets.net

National Minimum Wage Helpline: 0845 600 0678

New Employers' Helpline: 0845 607 0143

Papworth Trust: www.papworth.org.uk

Part time workers' regulations: www.dti.gov.uk/er/ptime.htm

Rare Breeds Survival Trust: www.rare-breeds.com

The Small Business Service: www.business.link.gov.uk

VAT Helpline: 0845 010 9000

W.I. Markets: www.wimarkets.co.uk

Bibliography

Small Business Co.UK, *Caterer and Hotelkeeper*, www.foodreference.com, www.datamonitor.com, *Eating British 2004, British Cheese Directory 2003, The British Regional Food and Drink Guide, The Observer, Observer Food Magazine, Evening Standard, The Guardian,* The *Times*, Food Standards Agency, The Papworth Trust, The Home Office, The Inland Revenue, HM Custom and Excise, The Immigration Service, Department of Trade and Industry, *In Business* (BBC Radio Four), The Food Programme (Radio 4), *Yellow Pages*, Federation of Small Businesses, British Chamber of Commerce, Brake Catering.

Barrow, Colin *Starting a Business For Dummies* (2004) John Wiley & Sons, Ltd.

Beckett, Fiona *Wine by Style* (1998) Mitchell Beazley.

Conway, Des *The Event Manager's Bible* (2004) How To Books.

Curnonsky (Maurice Sailland) *The Larousse Traditional French Cookery* (1987) Ebury Press.

Erdosh, George *Start & Run a Catering Business* (2001) Self-Counsel.

Grant, Amanda *Lunchbox* (1999) Prion.

Gray, Patience *Honey From a Weed* (1986) Prospect Books.

Gray, Rose and Rogers, Ruth *River Café Cook Book Green* (2000) Ebury Press.

Grigson, Sophie *Sophie Grigson's Herbs* (1999) BBC.

Johnson-Bell, Linda *Good Food Fine Wine* (1999) Cassell.

Ladenis, Nico *My Gastronomy* (1987) Ebury Press.

Lillicrap, Dennis, Cousins, John and Smith, Robert *Food and Beverage Service* (1998) Hodder & Stoughton.

Stewart, Katie *The Sociable Cook* (2001) BBC Worldwide Limited.

Little, Alastair *Keep It Simple* (1993) Conran Octopus.

Price, Alison *Perfect Parties* (1999) Kyle Cathie Limited.

Price, Alison *Weddings* (2001) Kyle Cathie Limited.

Richards, Judy *Start and Run a Money-Making Business – Catering* (1994) McGraw-Hill.

Riley, Michael *Managing People* (2000) Butterworth Heinemann.

Tyrer, Polly *Party Pieces* (1986) Little, Brown and Company.

Roux, Albert and Roux, Michel *New Classic Cuisine* (1983) Macdonald.

Weller, Lyn *Health & Vitality Cookbook* (2000) Harper Collins.

Index

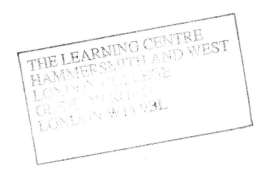